PRAISE FOR GENERATIONS OF GRIEF

"Tammy Cortez gives voice to the often invisible grief experienced by caregivers. *Generations of Grief* is an honest, tender reflection on what it means to love someone through loss, and how we begin to carry both memory and healing. "
—**Christina Rasmussen**, Bestselling Author of *Invisible Loss*

"Tammy masterfully weaves a poignant narrative that transcends the individual experience of loss and delves deeply into how grief ripples through an entire family. This book is a heartfelt exploration of the complexities of familial bonds under the weight of grief, offering readers both comfort and insight. *Generations of Grief* offers hope, understanding, and a compassionate look at how we can support one another in the face of heartache. "
—**Margo LaBerge**, Life Tribute Professional, Author of *Living Life with Gusto*

"Before reading Tammy's Generations of Grief, I viewed grief like an annoying cut—something you just have to deal with until it heals. I now realize it's not something I wait for to go away; it's something I learn to carry."

—**Michael Jaymes**

"Alzheimer's is a thief. It robs you of bits and pieces of the one you love. With each loss comes moments of grief. Tammy's book gives us permission to look into the mirror, see the grief, name it, and understand that this is all part of being on the other side of dementia. "

—**Myrna Marofsky**, Author of *To The Last Dance: A Partner's Story of Living and Loving Through Dementia*

"In hearing of this lifework that wrote itself through the raw stages of grief, it shouldn't surprise me that Tammy has turned her pain into something that will help others.

This intelligently written collection of tools, with practical applications for moving past heartache, will help you emerge on the other side better for having loved—and hurt—to thrive and become your authentic self.

Nowhere on the shelves of bookstores will you find a more comprehensive plan to heal—refreshing in a world that promotes masking emotions. If you want to become the best version of yourself while honoring the love you shared through loss, read this and anything you can get your hands on from this genuinely caring, well-read author.

If you are a professional in grief counseling, consider this work a resource for your staff. This refreshingly simple

approach to healing the void is exactly the way to pave that path.
You are now on your way to healing! "

—**Dawn DeBiase Volt**, Self-Proclaimed Empath Extraordinaire

"This chapter gives a heartwarming look into the connections we maintain with our lost loved ones, showing evidence of grief theory in action. "

—**Jenni Schulz, PhD, MSW, LSW**, Adjunct Professor of Social Work & Psychology

GENERATIONS OF GRIEF:

Embracing Change Through Loss

GENERATIONS OF GRIEF:

Embracing Change Through Loss

A reflective book/journal on grief

———————

Tammy Cortez

A TLC PUBLISHING STUDIO BOOK

GENERATIONS OF GRIEF: EMBRACING CHANGE THROUGH LOSS

Copyright © 2025 by Tammy Cortez

All rights reserved. No part of this publication may be reproduced, distributed, or transmitted in any form or by any means—including photocopying, recording, storing, or other electronic or mechanical methods—without the prior written permission of the author, except in the case of brief quotations used in reviews, academic citations, or other permitted noncommercial uses under U.S. copyright law.

All images, logos, quotes, and trademarks referenced in this book remain the property of their respective owners and are used in accordance with U.S. trademark and copyright regulations.

ISBN: 979-8-9987499-0-2 (Hardcover)
ISBN: 979-8-9987499-1-9 (Keepsake Edition – Available at www.TammyLCortez.com or select events)
Published by TLC Publishing Studio

Las Vegas, Nevada
www.TLCJobPath.com

Printed in the United States of America

Disclaimer

This book is intended for informational and inspirational purposes only and is not a substitute for professional advice, diagnosis, or treatment. The author is not a licensed medical or mental health professional. Always seek the advice of a qualified provider with any questions you may have regarding grief, trauma, or other medical or psychological conditions. Never disregard professional medical advice or delay seeking it because of something you read in this book.

The author and publisher have made every effort to ensure the accuracy of the information presented. Any names, locations, or details resembling real individuals are used with permission or have been changed to protect privacy. The inclusion of resources or third-party references does not imply endorsement and third party content remains their rights. The author and publisher assume no responsibility or liability for errors, omissions, or how this material is used by readers.

DEDICATION

To my mom, the strongest woman I know: I hope this book brings you comfort and peace, offering guidance as you navigate grief and the journey we are all learning to walk together. Your resilience and love have been a constant source of strength for me, my brothers, and everyone closest to us.

My deepest hope is that these words bring healing in those times when sorrow feels overwhelming. May this book be a steady companion, a reminder of our shared love and a source of support whenever you need it. Let it serve as a stepping stone toward finding hope and peace as you continue moving forward with all of us by your side.

Thank you for sharing your personal journal with me, allowing this book to reach its full potential. Your selflessness, resilience, and unwavering power to continue inspire me. You are an incredible and beautiful person, and I am endlessly grateful for you.

To my brothers: Your unwavering presence and strength continue to bring peace of mind as we navigate this uncharted path together. As long as we move forward together, we will be OK.

To my husband: Thank you for allowing me to grieve in ways I never imagined would happen, for never passing judgment on my emotions that I couldn't fully explain. I appreciate you more than I can ever explain. You are my world, my partner, and my strength. Through every challenge, high and low, you have stood by my side with steadfast love and patience.

Your support continues to carry us through the hardest days, lifting our family up in times of need. This book is a testament to your love and faith in me and us. Just as you have always been there for me, I am here for you, always. Love always and forever, xoxo.

To my children: Never let anyone dictate how you should grieve! Only you understand the depth of your feelings. Express them in whatever way feels right and safe for you, and those around you. Remember, family is everything. Don't worry about the small things that can get blown out of proportion. Hold on to the traditions, the memories, and the love that you have cherished over the years. Take those memories and let them guide you forward.

To my close family and friends: Your encouragement, understanding, and compassion have been a cornerstone of my force during this journey. Thank you for listening, holding space for me, and believing in me when I needed it most. Your presence has been a sincere gift, and I only hope I can do the same for you.

To those grieving any kind of loss: Whether this is a new experience for you or a familiar one, the steps you take must be in your own time and on your own terms. No one can tell you when it's time to move forward, but I hope in sharing my story, you find some comfort in knowing you are not alone. Many have walked this road before and understand the weight of this journey.

For me, this book may be the first step toward healing. By sharing my story and my grief over the loss of my dad, I hope to help you find the courage to take your first step forward. May these pages inspire you to cherish the love and memories of those you've lost, holding them close as you navigate your own path.

Need Help?

If grief becomes overwhelming and you need immediate support, reach out for help.

National Suicide Prevention Lifeline:

1-800-273-8255

or

https://suicidepreventionlifeline.org/

TABLE OF CONTENTS

Praise for Generations of Grief i
Generations of Grief: v
Generations of Grief: Embracing Change Through Loss vii
Dedication i
Table of Contents iii
Anecdote vii
Preface ix
Chapter One 1
My Parents and Our Last Trip 1
    Reflecting on Early Grief 2
    The Disney Cruise 3
    Grief Reflection: Moving Beyond the "What-Ifs" 8
    Exercise: Reflecting on Your Own Grief Journey 8

Chapter Two The Unexpected 11
    Diagnosis and Deterioration 12
    Coming to Terms – Anticipatory Grief 14
    Exercise: Reflecting on Grief 18
    My Reflection 18

Chapter Three Taking Care of Dad 21
    Hallucinations and the Final Days 21
    Navigating Family Emotions 23
    Reflecting on Grief: Seven Stages of Grief 25
    Exercise: Reflecting on Grief 26

Chapter Four Final Time Together 31

    Family Departures 31
    Moments of Joy and Sorrow 32
    Recollections of Papa 33
    Dad's Final Days 34
    Exercise: Reflecting on Grief 39

Chapter Five The Start of Life After 41
    Revisiting the Journal 41
    Struggles with Guilt and Helplessness 42
    Comfort in Family Togetherness 47
    Finding Nothing on the Shelf 48
    Grieving Through the Lens 49
    Mom's Reflections on Loneliness 50
    Dream Visitations and Next Steps 59
    Understanding the Stages of Grief 60
    Exercise: Reflecting on Your Grief Journey 61

Chapter Six The Impact of Past Grief 65
    Understanding Compounded Grief 68
    Exercise: Unpacking Layered Grief 69

Chapter Seven The Emotion of It All 73
    Respecting Everyone's Grief 73
    The Impact of Grief on Children 75
    Ways to Help a Child Cope with Grief 76
    Additional Tips for Grieving Together 77
    Exercise: Understanding the Emotional Layers of Grief ... 80

Chapter Eight Stepping Forward 85
    Evolving Grief 87
    Honoring Traditions 90
    Embracing Joy Without Guilt 90
    Exercise: Learning to Carry Grief 91

Chapter Nine What to Remember 95

Resources for Support	108
Grief Support Groups	109
Online Resources and Articles	109
Therapy and Counseling	109
Journaling and Personal Reflection	109
Personal Reflections	110

Chapter Ten The Power of Journaling 111

Part 1 – As Death Approaches	112
Legal Documents	113
Financial Documents	113
Property and Assets	114
Health and Medical Information	114
Digital Information	114
Personal Preferences	115
Final Arrangements	115
Important Contacts	116
Part 2: Journal – Starting Your Reflection	117
Reflection Prompts	117
Until We Meet Again	120

Chapter Eleven Conclusion 123

My Letter to My Dad	123

Chapter Twelve Acknowledgment 125

Special Supporters	126
Executive Contributor	127

Reflections Through Writing A Guide to Your Journaling Memories 129

What Comes After the Journal	130

Your Journal 131

References 339

Research and Educational Sources	339

Grief Support and Online Communities............................340
Therapy and Immediate Support......................................340
Tools and Resources 340
Personal Contributions...341
Note on Resources and Acknowledgments.......................341

About The Author...345
Also Available..346
Connect with Me 347

ANECDOTE

I'll never forget the second I saw the doctor's expression shift. They entered the hospital room clutching a clipboard, lips pressed into a thin line, and in that instant, my heart lurched. Dad lay in the bed, eyes fixed on the ceiling as though searching for something, or someone, just out of reach. I glanced over at Mom, who was standing next to me leaning on the doorway entrance almost as if she were using the doorway for support. The words "stage 4 lung cancer" felt like a sledgehammer to my chest, compounding the agony of his Alzheimer's diagnosis. My legs wobbled, and for a second, I forgot how to breathe. It didn't matter how many times I'd told myself to be strong; nothing could prepare me for the reality that my father's life had been turned upside down for the second time.

In that surreal haze of beeping monitors and fluorescent lights, I realized our roles had shifted. I was no longer just a daughter! I was about to take over my Mother's role and become Dad's caregiver for the next two weeks, Mom's rock, and my own harshest critic in the days to come. That hospital room became the epicenter of everything I never wanted to face, yet I somehow knew I had to.

PREFACE

I wish I could tell you that moment was the only second of disbelief, but it was just the beginning. Loss can unravel your world in a heartbeat. When my father was diagnosed with Alzheimer's, the changes in his health slowly began to reshape our reality. Watching him decline was heartbreaking. But watching my mother lose her best friend and husband of fifty years broke something different. It was this emotion of grief and of loss that compelled me to write.

This book began as a way to understand my heartache, but it became something more. It's a reflection not just of my experience, but of a passage many of us take. One that we rarely talk about yet silently carry. This is not a story about cancer; it's a story about love, memory, heartbreak, and the quiet strength we find in the middle of it all.

Even now, I struggle to accept the reality that my dad is gone. Just writing those words shakes me more than I ever imagined possible. You think you can prepare, try to plan, and brace yourself, but nothing can truly prepare you.

It's been just over a month since we said goodbye, and I'm still learning how to move forward while holding on to everything he meant to us.

Grief isn't easy. It doesn't arrive with a manual. My hope in writing this book is that, on your hardest days, these pages bring you even a small sense of comfort. Maybe it's something you reach for when you're trying to get out of bed, or when you finally admit, "I cried today," or "I don't know what to do next." If you're in that space right now, I want you to know: You don't need to have it all figured out. I don't either. But if we take it one day at a time, we may find we're stronger than we ever imagined.

If you've ever felt helpless watching someone you love slip away—this book is for you.

The title *Generations of Grief* came to me when I realized how long grief had been quietly shaping our lives. Alzheimer's brings loss long before the final goodbye. We grieved as Dad slowly faded from the person we knew, and we struggled to find accessible resources and support—especially for my mom. That search led to the early idea for a website: a space where people could find guidance, share their experiences, and feel a little less alone.

But as I worked on that site, life changed. The doctor shared news that added another layer of complexity to Dad's journey—one that no family is ever truly prepared for. The weight of two terminal diagnoses was more than we knew how to carry. I was focused on helping Mom understand what Dad was facing, but I didn't realize until later how much support I needed, too. Grief crept in long before his death and it stayed long after.

We often avoid talking about grief—trying to fix it, quiet it, rush it. But that's not how grief works. Whether you've lost someone to illness, miscarriage, a health crisis, or something else entirely, grief is complicated. Tangled. Unpredictable. And yet, through it all, we carry the people we love forward with us.

I began this book in the wake of my dad's passing, and now, more than two years later, life has shifted again. I find myself facing more heartache—this time with two other family members walking their own health journeys. Grief doesn't end; it evolves. It slips back into our lives unexpectedly, reshaping how we see the world and ourselves—then, now, and in the future.

Please know, I'm not a licensed counselor or therapist. What I've shared in these pages comes from my lived experience. If you need more support, I encourage you to speak with a professional who can walk with you through your pain. What I *can* offer you is honesty. The kind that says:

"You don't have to be ok today." The kind that reminds you—you're not alone in this.

This book is a companion for those navigating grief in all its forms. Through stories, reflections, and gentle exercises, I hope you find space to breathe, cry, reflect, and even smile again. Heartaches change us, but they also teach us how deeply we've loved.

May this journey help you carry your grief with grace, honor your memories with love, and take each step forward—at your own pace, in your own way.

—Tammy Cortez

You don't have to face it alone.

CHAPTER ONE

MY PARENTS AND OUR LAST TRIP

Grief comes in many forms, and it often begins long before the actual loss. For me, it started when I watched my father's vibrant personality gradually give way to the effects of Alzheimer's. Each small change felt like losing a piece of him, long before his final goodbye. Ironically, Alzheimer's would not be the cause of his death, and what lay ahead would challenge everything I thought I knew about love, loss, and the importance of being present.

As my parents navigated the daily challenges of his illness, my mom clung to the belief that every remaining instant was worth celebrating. She knew time was slipping away and wanted to make the most of it while Dad could still grasp the significance of certain milestones. That's when she called me.

"Your dad and I have our fiftieth wedding anniversary coming up," she said. "I want to celebrate early by going on a Disney Cruise for three or four days. I don't think he can handle more than that, and I'd love for all of you to join us. It might be our last trip together."

Her request was bittersweet. My parents had spent their lives traveling, taking us on childhood adventures and later exploring the world with friends and family. They had just returned from a three-week trip to France with my brother, his wife, and friends. During that trip, Dad had fallen. Though he was OK, it was a wake-up call. His Alzheimer's was worsening, and my mom was starting to see it, too.

A tug-of-war unfolded within me. I was unemployed and job hunting. What if I received an offer before the trip? Would taking time off jeopardize my chances? Ultimately, I decided that if a job couldn't understand our family's situation, it wasn't right for me. I didn't want to have regrets. My mom reached out to my brothers and relatives, and soon, ten or twelve of us were set to gather for what felt like the final chapter of a long, shared story.

REFLECTING ON EARLY GRIEF

Grief doesn't always wait for loss. Since Dad's passing, I've often wondered how I would have felt if I hadn't joined them on that trip. Even though I did go, guilt still crept in—guilt for even considering not going. What I didn't realize at the time was that I was already grieving. **Anticipatory grief**, the sadness you feel when you know a loss is coming but it hasn't happened yet, had begun to take root. I noticed it during phone calls, when I paused and wondered if this would be the last time I heard his voice. Or when I lingered over old family photos, feeling something, I couldn't yet name.

Grief doesn't follow a neat path. It can begin long before the final goodbye. That was my first lesson: Grief starts before you think it does. Journaling and acknowledging those feelings helped me lift some of that early weight.

Reflect: When have you experienced that quiet, persistent sadness before a loss was fully realized? Recognizing this early sorrow can be the first step toward healing.

THE DISNEY CRUISE

Once we confirmed our plans, I made it my mission to simplify the travel experience for my parents. Aware that Mom was shouldering the heavy burden of caregiving, I spoke to her about flying semiprivate to avoid crowded airports and choosing a hotel near the cruise terminal. My parents had always been seasoned travelers; Dad even worked in the airline industry his whole life. I knew they'd handle most details gracefully, but this time felt different. I just wanted to make things as effortless as possible, especially for Mom.

When we all met in San Diego, Mom shared how smoothly their flight had gone. The semiprivate experience proved worthwhile, with staff who were attentive and patient. Alzheimer's had taken away much of Dad's independence; he often became disoriented. Seeing him after months apart brought reality crashing down on me like a wave. His once-steady hands trembled, and his distant gaze hinted at the mental fog that Alzheimer's brings. Although Mom had warned me about his decline, living in a different state meant I hadn't seen the changes firsthand. Nothing could have prepared me for how much he had changed. He was unsteady, unsure of his steps, but he was still the loving father I knew, deeply devoted to Mom. He had always been a strong man with a booming voice, a rock in our family. Now, I saw someone more fragile, but no less full of love. He was still looking at my mom with devotion and care in his eyes.

We spent the next few days celebrating my parents' fiftieth anniversary. I wasn't sure how much he understood, yet he still held Mom's hand and kissed her on the lips like he always had throughout their decades of marriage. Even Alzheimer's couldn't take away that loving habit.

One night, Dad woke up confused and wandered from the cabin. Thankfully, Mom noticed right away, and my brother found him wandering the halls. The thought of him ending up on the wrong floor chilled us. From that point on, Mom chose to stay on the ship and even placed luggage in front of the cabin door to wake her if it happened again. She wore a calm face, determined to make the most of our fleeting time together.

We also celebrated anniversaries, and birthdays, including Dad's. He was a Halloween baby, and in our family, that's always a big deal. My husband dressed him in a festive Halloween blazer, and for a flash, his old confident smile returned. I played Connect Four with Dad—his eyes lit up with each win, though the clarity faded within minutes. Alzheimer's is cruel like that, offering brief glimpses of the person you love, only to snatch them away again. Still, I cherished every flicker of recognition.

I want to pause to share two of my favorite photos from the cruise: one of Dad in that Halloween jacket, and another of my parents holding hands at dinner, smiling. If I can offer a piece of advice, it's this: Take the pictures. Capture every moment. Those images will become treasures.

.

Dad on the cruise in my husband's Halloween jacket

MY PARENTS ON THE CRUISE PRIOR TO DINNER

Our time together was filled with laughter, honest conversations, and the steady pulse of a family determined to hold on to every second. I was so grateful for the chance to be there. That cruise was more than a trip; it was a gift.

Each time, I felt both anguish for what we were losing and gratitude for what still remained. Little did I know how much more we would lose in the coming months.

GRIEF REFLECTION: MOVING BEYOND THE "WHAT-IFS"

Remember, you cannot live in the past. The endless "what-ifs and should-haves" can trap you in regret. Instead, treasure your memories in a way that honors love rather than guilt. In the early stages of grief, it's natural to blame yourself. But dwelling on what might have been only prevents you from being fully present.

EXERCISE: REFLECTING ON YOUR OWN GRIEF JOURNEY

Use the space below or the journal section of this book to explore your own story.

1. **Identify a Memory**: Choose an experience with your loved one—big or small.
2. **Write It Down**: Describe it in detail. What did you feel? What made it meaningful?

3. **Embrace the Emotions**: Let yourself feel joy, sorrow, anger, or guilt. All are valid.
4. **Release the Guilt**: When you finish, breathe deeply. Acknowledge any guilt, but don't let it linger. The past can't be changed—but you can choose how to move forward.

Date

___

Begin here. There's strength in sharing your first steps.

This is just one step, but it matters. I'm learning that grief is a constant companion. It arrives in waves—bringing guilt, regret, and the echo of "what if." One of the hardest lessons I've had to learn is not letting self-pity take root. Instead of dwelling on the "should-haves or could-haves" I focus on the recollections I did have. By holding on to those memories with love instead of regret, we honor the past while continuing forward.

As the cruise ended and I returned to my day-to-day life, I couldn't shake the feeling that something larger loomed on the horizon. I didn't know then how quickly the next phone call would upend our world and draw us into a chapter none of us was ready for.

CHAPTER TWO

THE UNEXPECTED

Two weeks after our trip, my mom called. Her trembling voice said everything before words even formed. My heart sank as I braced myself for bad news. She told me Dad had been losing weight rapidly and wasn't eating. His doctor had recommended immediate hospitalization for further evaluation. Though she didn't directly ask me to come down to Arizona, I heard the unspoken plea in her voice. Without hesitation, I packed a bag and headed to be with them.

Seeing Dad in a hospital bed was heartbreaking in ways I hadn't expected. The clarity he'd shown on the cruise had already begun to fade. He was frail—his sturdy frame diminished, his voice faint. Mom held his hand and whispered reassurances with gentle calm. Nurses encouraged him to walk with their help, but he still refused most food. Over the next few days, I managed to coax him into eating three or four pieces of banana, a couple spoonfuls of yogurt, and some water, but it wasn't enough to sustain him. His condition showed no signs of improvement.

The following days blurred together: tests, uncertainty, and the agonizing pain of watching Dad decline rapidly. I recall Dad pointing toward a corner of the hospital room and saying someone was standing there. My stomach dropped as I realized he was referring to a blue strap hanging from the cabinet. I gently walked over and removed it. As soon as it was gone, his body relaxed. For a fleeting moment, peace returned to his face. But the hallucinations continued. One day, in a soft and strangely serene voice, he spoke of pearly gates and the sound of trumpets. My heart tightened as I asked if he saw his parents. He quietly shook his head. This pattern was repeated not only with me, but also during conversations with my brother. It left me wondering: Was he caught between two worlds? Were we witnessing something beyond our understanding? Those moments were haunting and sacred.

DIAGNOSIS AND DETERIORATION

At first, the doctors thought it was pneumonia, but something didn't sit right with me. I felt the weight of the situation settle heavily in my chest. Trying to stay proactive, I turned to Mom and suggested, "Let's get you a journal. The doctors are going to give us a lot of information. We'll need to keep track of it all." She agreed. We briefly stepped out for lunch and picked up a journal.

I remember rushing back to the hospital, my heart pounding, and seeing the agony and nervousness etched into Mom's face. It was like fate was waiting behind that hospital door—something we didn't want to hear, but knew we needed to in order to move forward. She clutched the journal in her lap as we drove, her hands gently trembling around its small cover. It felt tiny in her grip, yet somehow monumental. On the first page, I had written a quote from Alex MacLean and a message from my husband and me:

Mom,

"Those we love don't go away; they walk beside us every day—unseen, unheard, but always near. Still loved, still missed, and very dear."

We love you so much. Please take the time to write out your thoughts, feelings, emotions, and anything else you need.

All our love.

I dated it **11/21/2022**. Little did I know how drastically our lives would change in just eight days.

When we returned to the hospital, the doctor was already waiting by Dad's bedside. This time it was unusually quiet, almost like the air was holding its breath. The doctor looked at us and said words that would forever alter our world: "It's not pneumonia. It's fluid around the lung."

The scan was brought over, and I stared at it, my mind racing. Then came the devastating diagnosis: **stage 4 lung cancer**. The ground shifted beneath me. Dad, already battling Alzheimer's, now faced an even more unrelenting fight. The cancer had metastasized. There were no treatment options left. Only hospice.

Though the staff spoke with care, that word—**hospice**—felt so final. Like a door quietly closing.

A cold wave washed over me. My mind froze, and I blurted, "What? I'm sorry, could you repeat that?" Part of me hoped that hearing it again would make it less real.

The doctor repeated, "Stage 4 lung cancer … and it has metastasized." Then, the most crushing blow: "A month or two." Just like that, our time together was no longer measured in years but in weeks.

My mom turned pale. Her shock and heartbreak mirrored my own. I felt frozen, unable to process how quickly everything had changed. I grabbed the journal and wrote down everything the doctor said, knowing we wouldn't remember otherwise.

COMING TO TERMS – ANTICIPATORY GRIEF

Grief rarely feels logical. I remember sitting in the hospital hallway, numb and unable to cry, even as my heart broke.

Denial and disbelief swirled inside me. How could this be happening? We had just celebrated his birthday.

Watching Mom absorb the news was even harder. She remained outwardly strong, asking questions, tending to Dad. But later, she broke down. Through quiet sobs, she whispered, "I don't know how to do this without him." I didn't have any answers. All I could do was hold her hand and sit with her pain.

Later, I learned her journal had become her refuge. When I began writing this book, she entrusted me with her most private thoughts, allowing me to glimpse the depths of her heart on those deeply personal pages. With her permission, I'm sharing a few excerpts here. These entries remain untouched, preserving their raw emotion and reminding us that in instances like these, grammar and structure lose their importance in comparison to the truth of our feelings.

Mom, thank you for your courage, your vulnerability, and your willingness to share your soul in this way.

Mom's Journal Entry – Tuesday 11/15/22

"He goes to the bathroom every few minutes. He thinks he's sneaking, and I don't see him, which makes me laugh. He still isn't eating anything except cookies. My son says to

give him whatever he wants at this point to help him gain weight. I agree.

He came into the kitchen and wanted to dance and always said, 'Did I tell you I love you?' and I say, 'No,' then he says, 'I do.' Every woman on earth should be so lucky. I try to keep from crying.

That evening, he wanted cookies, and I got them for him. I often wonder how long I have with him."

Mom's Journal Entry (Partial) – Thursday 11/17/22

"Went to McDonald's as he wanted a cheeseburger. While we were there, the doctor's office called and said they wanted him to go to the ER directly. They would call ahead.

We went and stayed late. He weighs 155 lbs. All the tests were done, and they said he has pneumonia. WHAT! They transferred him to a room. Finally left at 12:30 a.m.

When I walked out, I felt this lonely feeling. The partner I laid next to all these years was going away."

Mom's Journal Entry – Saturday 11/19/22

"Today is Saturday. Tammy comes home, and I could have cried when I saw her. It was such a relief for me."

Even though Dad was still alive, mourning had already begun. Reading Mom's words confirmed it; we were both grieving before the end came. That's **anticipatory grief**, mourning the life you knew while it's still unfolding in front of you. Grief isn't linear. It doesn't wait for the final goodbye. It can sneak in early, quietly growing heavier with every change, every decline, every moment that feels like the last.

The five stages of grief are commonly known: denial, anger, bargaining, depression, and acceptance. Some models describe seven stages: shock, denial, anger, bargaining, depression, testing, and acceptance. These stages don't follow a tidy order and not everyone experiences them the same way. But understanding them helps us name what we feel, even in the most uncertain moments.

EXERCISE: REFLECTING ON GRIEF

1. **Journal Exercise**: Write down how you're feeling right now. Is there a particular stage of grief that resonates with you? It doesn't need to make sense. Just let your thoughts flow.
2. **Memory Reflection**: Recall a moment with your loved one that brings you joy. What did it teach you about love, life, or even loss? Write it out in as much detail as you can.

MY REFLECTION

One recollection that always brings me comfort is the time Dad and I were on the deck of the cruise at night just before the fireworks were to go off. The air was still warm, and the night sky was full of stars. He looked at me and winked like he had when I was little. We didn't talk much, but that silence was full of understanding. In that quiet moment, I felt wrapped in his presence and strength. It reminded me that love doesn't always need words; it shows up in presence, in tradition, in stillness. That memory reminds me I'm not alone in my sadness; he's still with me, in every clear night and with every star I see.

There is no right answer and no fixed timeline. Grief is personal, layered, and ever-changing. Let yourself be where you are.

Date

This space is for your truth—no filter, no judgment.

Date

Standing in the hallway outside Dad's hospital room, I barely had time to catch my breath before reality came crashing down. Little did I know the hardest part was still to come or that our family would be tested in ways we never imagined.

CHAPTER THREE

TAKING CARE OF DAD

Once the doctors and Mom agreed there was nothing more that could be done, we realized that the cancer had advanced too far. Her only wish was for Dad to spend his final days at home. He was released from the hospital and placed under hospice care, and everything happened so quickly. Within days, he went from full conversations and soft mentions of pearly gates and trumpets to being home with us, surrounded by love.

HALLUCINATIONS AND THE FINAL DAYS

This isn't about religion or beliefs—this was simply our reality. When the doctors confirmed we were no longer pursuing treatment and I heard Dad talk about those gates, something in me shifted. A gut feeling told me the doctor's timeline was too generous. I told Mom I thought we only had two weeks, at most. I wasn't a doctor, but I needed to prepare her—prepare us. It was one of the hardest conversations I've ever had, but I know now it was the right one.

Mom's Journal Entry (Before Dad Came Home) – Wednesday 11/23/22

"My dear husband was doing much better today. He had some visitors, and that seemed to perk him up. He still won't eat, and there's no change from the doctor.

I kept hoping they'd tell me this was all a mistake. How can this be? I never thought I'd lose him to cancer. I barely slept last night.

Thank God for my kids; without them, I wouldn't go on. I worry they'll get busy with their lives and forget about me, but deep down, I know they won't.

I wonder how it will be when everyone leaves, and my love is gone. What then?"

The confusion we all felt was very consuming. Mom had already taken care of many legal matters, power of attorney, their family trust, but we hadn't prepared emotionally. Organizing funeral arrangements, notifying everyone, and confronting the reality of impending loss all hit us at once. We thought we had more time, but reality was relentless and coming full force.

Mom's Journal Entry – Thursday 11/24/22

"Today, my son and I went to see him. He talked a lot to him. He was so animated with his hands. They both talked about aviation. You could tell he was excited to talk to him. You could see the love between them. I kept asking my son what he was saying because I couldn't understand him.

Called hospice, but with the holiday coming up, they told me to call back in the morning."

Dad came home the day before Thanksgiving. By then, my brothers and I had gathered at our parents' house with our families. It was a bittersweet reunion.

NAVIGATING FAMILY EMOTIONS

We all knew our time was limited. We smiled, held hands, took photos, and soaked in every precious second. Hospice delivered a bed, oxygen, and medication to be administered every four hours. I took on the responsibility.

Giving Dad his medication was one of the most painful roles I've ever had. It tore me up inside. At first, I could feel how he responded to me, still aware, still present. But over time, his swallowing weakened, and I had to be so careful not to make him choke. What once took thirty seconds eventually stretched into fifteen minutes, placing medication gently into the side of his cheek, letting it absorb slowly into his system. Each dose became a quiet reminder of how much he was fading. Toward the end, I remember one dose in particular; he started to choke, just as the hospice nurse had warned might happen. Even though I had been told what to do—raise his bed up—it terrified me. Dad was preparing to leave us, and yet I was terrified I might cause more harm than good.

Still, I knew I couldn't let Mom do it. I wanted to protect her from the emotional scars I knew I'd carry forever. I wanted her memories to be filled with warmth, not worry. Over time, she began to step back during those moments. And I often thought, "I'm so glad she's not the one doing this," because with every dose, I could feel him slipping further away.

During those days, I felt compelled to take photos of Dad. It wasn't easy. It felt like a necessary way to process the changes. Through the lens, I could step back just enough to see what was happening. Like holding up a mirror to grief, the photos became a quiet record of the changes in his body and spirit. I've never shown anyone the final photos, even when asked—especially not Mom. She asked me many times, and each time, I gently declined. Years later, she thanked me for not showing her.

As the days passed, the signs of Dad's decline became harder to ignore. Three days before he passed, my niece and nephew were at the house. My nephew suddenly said, "Oh, I'm sorry, I didn't see you there." When Mom asked who he was talking to, he described a woman—my grandmother. Later, my niece said she saw the same woman standing by the door. No matter your beliefs, moments like that make you wonder. We all felt it: Dad's time was near.

REFLECTING ON GRIEF: SEVEN STAGES OF GRIEF

As we've touched on, grief is not linear. It's messy. It's layered. It doesn't follow a script.

These are the seven stages often used to describe grief:

1. **Shock** – the initial numbness or disbelief
2. **Denial** – rejecting the reality of the loss
3. **Anger** – frustration or helplessness, often without a clear target
4. **Bargaining** – thoughts of "what if" or "if only"
5. **Depression** – the heaviness of sadness and despair
6. **Testing** – trying to find new ways to cope
7. **Acceptance** – acknowledging the reality and learning how to live with it

I experienced many of these before Dad even passed and again after. The shock of the diagnosis. The denial of how fast it all happened. The anger, not at anyone, but at the unfairness of it. The bargaining—had I done enough, could I do something more? Depression settled in as we watched him fade. Testing came through care, photos, journaling—any way I could cope. Acceptance doesn't mean the sting goes away or that you are over it; it just means you are learning how to live with the loss.

EXERCISE: REFLECTING ON GRIEF

Take a few quiet moments to reflect on where you are in your own grief.

1. **Journal Exercise**: What stage or stages resonate with you right now? Write honestly. Let it flow, no matter how messy.
2. **Memory Reflection**: Recall a meaningful moment with your loved one. What did it teach you? Capture it in writing. Let the memory stay with you.

As you work through these stages, remember that there's no correct pace. This is personal, complex, and unpredictable. What matters is allowing yourself to feel, learn, and heal in your own time.

27 | TAKING CARE OF DAD

Date

Date

We were doing our best to keep steady, to make peace with our routine. But peace was fragile. Just as we began to breathe through the rhythm of caregiving, life reminded us that grief rarely follows a script. I thought the hardest days might be behind us. I was wrong. What came next would demand more of us than I ever imagined I could give.

CHAPTER FOUR

FINAL TIME TOGETHER

After Thanksgiving, my brother and his family, along with my husband, returned home, leaving the house eerily quiet. A deep, unsettling silence settled in. The familiar hum of daily life, the shared laughter, the feeling of everyone rallying around Dad—had vanished. In its place was a stillness that made every room feel empty and forlorn. It was as if the house itself were mourning, amplifying the ache of loss and the heavy anticipation of what my mom and I now had to manage.

FAMILY DEPARTURES

Mom's Journal Entry – Saturday 11/26/22

"My son and his family left today. It was really hard! I hated to see him go. I think when he left, Dad took a turn.

Maybe he knows. I often wonder what he's thinking. I don't think he'll last much longer."

For most of those final days, it was just Mom, Dad, and me in the house. I vividly recall a conversation with Mom about Dad and his parents, a memory that stirred some of my favorite childhood moments, especially around the holidays. My dad always had a way of making every season magical. I remember snowy winters when the neighborhood kids would flock to our house to build giant snowmen with him, our yard transformed into a joyful hub of laughter.

MOMENTS OF JOY AND SORROW

No matter where we lived, Dad made every holiday unforgettable. On Halloween, we carved elaborate jack-o'-lanterns. Dad's was always the best. At Christmas, he lit up the house inside and out, stringing lights with my brothers and me. I still smile remembering the Folgers Coffee can filled with extra bulbs, always ready for a quick fix. "We must make sure the tree is completely covered with lights for Mom," he'd say, "because she wants it to look beautiful for us." Those memories, bittersweet now, brought light to our heavy present.

Visiting my grandparents' house was another source of joy. My cousins, brothers, and I spent hours running through the backyard. The real centerpiece, though, was the swing my grandfather hung between two trees, an apple and a cherry tree. That swing was magic. As I got older, I spent time there talking, laughing, and soaking up conversations that stayed with me. Now, I try to recapture that same magic in my own family traditions, like the wind chimes Dad loved so much. I hope those little things pass on a sense of wonder to the next generation.

While reminiscing, Mom mentioned that my grandparents' wedding anniversary was November 29. In that instant, I felt a deep, unshakable sense that Dad would pass on that day. We spoke about it briefly, then quietly returned our focus to his care.

RECOLLECTIONS OF PAPA

When my grandparents were alive, they visited us on the West Coast. I was pregnant with my second child and something unexpected happened. One night, my papa passed away suddenly during that trip. He was so much like my dad— strong, steady, and deeply loving—that losing him shook me. Still, I held back my grief, knowing I was preparing to bring new life into the world.

My nana was devastated, and the whole family felt the weight of the passing. I remember my aunt saying, "Tammy, can you hurry up and have this baby?" It startled me, but I knew she was just searching for hope. A week later, I gave birth to my daughter. As a tribute, I gave her a middle name that began with the same initial as Papa's—a quiet way to keep his memory close.

Grief is unpredictable. It doesn't ask permission. In those final days with Dad, I found myself treasuring the smallest moments.

DAD'S FINAL DAYS

I still remember Saturday mornings growing up, how Dad would wiggle my big toe and say, "Rise and shine, sleepyhead! Time to get up!" At the time, I dreaded it. Now, I'd give anything to hear it again.

Two days before he passed, I had a dream so vivid it felt like a visit. In it, Dad was wiggling my toe again, smiling. "Look, I'm OK," he said. "Nothing hurts. Don't worry, I didn't feel anything." When I woke up, I saw him resting in the hospice bed at the foot of the couch where I'd been sleeping. And I just knew he was preparing to go.

Mom's journal echoed the same feeling. She worried he knew it was time and wouldn't last much longer. The next day, I realized I hadn't taken a photo of him the day before. Mom urged me to take one. When I did, I saw how much he'd changed. I didn't show her—it was too final, too raw.

That evening, I told Mom, "We're really close. I don't think Dad will make it till tomorrow."

She asked, "How do you know?"

"I can see it in the photo," I whispered.

We both understood. We were losing my dad. She was losing her husband, her best friend, her life partner. We hoped he'd make it to the next day, his parents' anniversary, but we knew in our hearts, time was short.

Mom's Journal Entry – Sunday 11/27/22

"I was really surprised he's still here. I feel so bad for Tammy giving him his medicine. It's got to be so hard on her. She is my angel. He is about the same. His oxygen is in the low 62-82. The nurse can't get a blood pressure reading. For some reason he keeps hanging on. I told him he can go and find nana. I tell him every day I love him, and I'll be okay."

Mom's Journal Entry – Monday 11/28/22

"I was up all night with Tammy. She is so strong! He would be so proud of her, I know I am. I kept checking on him all night. I could just feel it in my heart." 😔

That final night was long. I kept giving Dad his medicine but chose not to sleep beside him in the living room. I wanted Mom to have that time with him. Instead, I slept in their bedroom and woke often. Around 2 a.m., an unsettling feeling stirred me. I stood quietly in the bedroom doorway, where I could see Dad resting in the living room. From there, I checked on him every twenty minutes, pacing softly through the hallway, doing my best not to disturb Mom while trying to calm my nerves. Something just felt off.

At 4 a.m., I finally told myself to rest for a little while. But just a short time later, about thirty minutes, Mom woke me in a panic: "I think Dad is gone."

Even before I checked his pulse, I knew. I clipped the monitor on his finger and glanced at the clock. It was 4:45 a.m.

Dad was gone!

Mom asked me to share the news with my siblings and other family members—a heartbreaking task. Yet it was even harder to watch my mom collapse into herself, unsure of what to do now that her life had changed forever.

Mom's Journal Entry – Tuesday 11/29/22

"Today is Tuesday at 5 a.m., and the love of my life went to heaven!

FINAL TIME TOGETHER | 37

God help me!

I woke Tammy and her brother, and we all cried.

How do you not, when he's always been there? He gave me the skills to survive. I told him, I love you, and I'll see you later. Save a place for me. I'm sure if he could have talked, he would have said, 'No problem, babe! Don't cry, I'll be with you always.'

LJ held on to him and cried so hard, for so long. That was so hard to see. Tammy was so strong. She held his hand and kissed him. She said she would call her older brother.

It was just so unbelievable to experience. The funeral director came and wrapped him up so nicely. I kissed him goodbye and said,

'Wait for me; I'll come soon.' 🙁

They took him and Tammy, and I went outside with him and watched the van leave. It felt like I was dreaming, an out-of-body experience. LJ couldn't watch. He was to upset. I feel for him.

The rest of the day is a blur ..."

In that moment, I understood something I hadn't before. I'd been grieving for weeks, feeling the sorrow of watching Dad decline. But now, I knew, this was real. This was final. Grief doesn't follow rules. It doesn't show up in order or on schedule. It crashes over you in waves, sometimes all at once, sometimes not at all. And that's OK.

Just before I gave him his final dose of medication, his eyes met mine. He didn't speak, but he didn't have to. There was something there—peace, maybe. Or a silent thank you. It was one of those fleeting memories you tuck away for life.

EXERCISE: REFLECTING ON GRIEF

Take a moment now to check in with yourself. Where are you in your process?

1. **Journal Your Feelings**: Write down what you're feeling today. Don't worry about grammar or structure; just let the words flow.

2. **Identify Your Stage**: Consider the stages of grief: shock, denial, anger, bargaining, depression, testing, acceptance. Which ones feel true to you right now?

3. **Revisit and Reflect**: Come back to this exercise in a few days or weeks. See what's shifted. Notice what's changed. Give yourself grace.

Grief doesn't follow a straight line. Let yourself feel what comes; trust that peace will return in time—even in the smallest, quietest ways.

Date

In the silence that followed, I thought we had entered a moment of calm. But what I didn't realize was that this was only the eye of the storm. The hardest days were still ahead.

CHAPTER FIVE

THE START OF LIFE AFTER

REVISITING THE JOURNAL

The journal I bought my mom to record doctor updates became a sanctuary, a place where she could pour her heart out and take tiny steps toward healing. In the weeks following Dad's passing, everything felt like a blur. It was hard to navigate my own emotions while focusing intently on my mom. Naturally, everyone's concern centered on her, which I understood. When you lose someone close, people often rally around the one left behind, perhaps as a way of offering comfort or a coping mechanism. While I can't say for certain why this happens, I can share what I experienced. But first, let me talk about Mom.

Her emotions were crushing, at times paralyzing. During deep grief, staying connected to family and friends is critical, not just for your own support, but also to uphold one another. As I mentioned earlier, Mom trusted me with her most private, heartfelt reflections, and through her words, I gained a deeper understanding of her emotional state. I've chosen to share some of those entries here because they highlight the importance of community and connection in the midst of loss. Heartbreak is personal, yet it's not meant to be carried alone.

STRUGGLES WITH GUILT AND HELPLESSNESS

By now, you've seen glimpses of Mom's journal, the private space where her grief poured out in real time. What I hadn't shared until now was just how much emotion it truly held. Her entries from those early days revealed a depth of heartbreak I hadn't fully understood until I found myself pausing again and again, not just to catch my breath, but to take in the depth of what she was experiencing.

Mom's Journal Entry – Wednesday 11/30/22

"I am so sad about my loss. I don't even know what to say. He was my everything. He was my strength. I looked up to him for guidance. He made me grow up and experience the world.

Every night he'd say, 'I love you a Bushell and a peck and I'd say a hug around the neck.' Every morning he'd say, 'I love you and hug me and say I'm so lucky to have you and you're the best thing that ever happened in my life.'

How can this be?

I'm not ready to let go yet ..."

This entry came early in her writing, and even now, it reads like both a love letter and a cry for help. Her words were raw, tangled in disbelief. She clung to the smallest rituals—his morning hugs, their bedtime exchanges—because those moments were what made their life feel full. Without them, she felt unanchored.

Mom's Journal Entry – Thursday 12/01/22

"Today is the day that Tammy leaves. I just want to fall to the ground and scream! She is the most wonderful child in the world. She took care of her dad til the very last moment.

I admire her strength! She loved him so much. She was his little girl, and he loved her.

I can't bare to see her leave. ☹"

Her entries shifted day by day, some filled with vivid memories, others barely more than a whisper of pain.

Mom's Journal Entry – Friday 12/02/22

"I cried!"

Mom's Journal Entry – Saturday 12/03/22

"I cried!"

Mom's Journal Entry – Sunday 12/04/22

"I cried! I don't think I can cry anymore."

The blur of time and misery made everything feel unreal. And yet, with every short entry, the finality of death crept in more deeply. It was as if the tears spoke louder than language ever could.

Mom's Journal Entry – Monday 12/05/22

"Today is my sister's birthday. I talked with her yesterday. It all seems like a blur.

This is the day they cremated my husband. How do you swallow that, it hurts to say that. So many nightmares!"

This one took my breath away. I remember that day vividly but reading her version of it pulled me into her heartache in a different way. The word *cremated* hit me with its finality. It wasn't just the act; it was the moment she realized he was really gone.

Mom's Journal Entry – Tuesday 12/06/22

"It's been one week since I lost my true love! It seems unbelievable! No one can ever prepare you for this.

It's awful!

I think back and ask, 'Did I say everything I wanted to say? Did he hear me when I told him I love him?' It feels like slow motion is happening. I miss him so much! Like I want to go back and have a moment in time with him.

I never thought it would happen so quick. NEVER!"

This entry broke my heart. That ache for just one more moment is something I think so many of us feel after loss. The questions we ask ourselves, Did I say enough? Did they know how deeply I loved them? These can become their own kind of torment. She wasn't only grieving his death—she was grieving every second they would never get back.

Mom's Journal Entry – Wednesday 12/07/22

"Another busy day which takes my mind off the sadness that I feel. Everyone is here, except for Tammy and her husband. Now I know why parents live next to their kids. I feel better when the house is full of family."

COMFORT IN FAMILY TOGETHERNESS

Though surrounded by family, her longing for wholeness remained. Grief has a way of highlighting what's missing, even in moments of togetherness. The quiet spaces left by Dad's absence echoed loudest in the small, everyday moments.

Even in heartache, she found moments of comfort in family togetherness. That small note about me and my husband missing from the gathering, it wasn't a complaint. It was just a mother missing the presence of her children. Her tenderness wasn't only about losing Dad; it was about longing to feel whole again.

After reading those entries, it's impossible not to feel the rawness of her anguish. Each word, whether a full paragraph or a simple "I cried," spoke volumes. These weren't just tears; they were pieces of a life unraveling. Through it all, I tried to show up for her the way she had always shown up for me. But in truth, inside I was drifting, unanchored and unsure of how to move forward. I felt like a shell of the daughter I'd always been, functioning on autopilot, quietly falling apart. I kept going through the motions, but part of me had disappeared the day he died.

I was completely lost.

The smallest things, a hummingbird outside the window, Dad's wind chimes stirring in the breeze, or the sight of an airplane, began to feel like signs. Each coincidence felt like a quiet reminder that Dad was still with us.

Our visit to the funeral home to set up Dad's cremation is something that will stay with me forever. I remember the distinctive smell as we walked in, stale and almost moldy, though I knew that wasn't what I was really smelling. It was the weight of finality. I tried to bring a little light to the moment, commenting on the beautiful pink flowers outside before we stepped in.

Inside, we were ushered into a quiet room where a long, narrow table covered with a black cloth stood. Lining the walls were five rows of urns—glass, marble, some with lights, some without. I hadn't realized how expensive they were. In that emotional state, every detail felt enormous, and it would've been easy to overspend trying to honor someone you love.

My mom was so fragile, and we were all doing our best to make decisions that honored my dad's wishes. He had asked for a simple cremation, nothing fancy. That's when I saw it: a small airplane necklace in one of the jewelry trays. It felt like a sign that everything would be OK.

Mom agreed with us that we would hold a celebration of life instead of a traditional funeral in February, just as Dad had wanted.

FINDING NOTHING ON THE SHELF

After returning home from the cremation arrangements, but before the celebration of life, I found myself at a bookstore, still searching for something to help me cope. I remember feeling almost embarrassed as I approached the counter and asked where to find books on grief. The clerk, who had been friendly, suddenly looked somber. He walked me to a tiny corner of the store, where a small shelf labeled "Death and Grieving" sat quietly in the back. Barely thirty inches wide. That moment made me furious and heartbroken all at once. In this day and age, how was this all we had? I started picking up each and every book, desperate for one that would connect with me, but nothing did. The emptiness of that shelf mirrored the emptiness I felt inside. I left the bookstore in tears and cried in my car—staring at the steering wheel, wondering why I felt even more lost than before I walked in.

GRIEVING THROUGH THE LENS

Building the video tribute for Dad's celebration of life was one of the hardest things I took on. I wanted to honor both him and my mom, but I didn't realize just how deeply it would reopen every wound. I often burst into tears unexpectedly, the kind of deep, painful sobbing that seizes your breath. Each photo brought a fresh wave of goodbye. I wondered how I could be grieving this intensely after all the sorrow I'd already experienced while caring for Dad. My husband noticed how physically drained I was—tense, restless, unable to focus. I hadn't realized how much I was holding in. Many times, I had to step away from the computer because I couldn't stop crying. I thought that eventually I'd grow numb to it after watching the clips over a hundred times. But I didn't. The agony stayed. This is when I started to learn that grief isn't a single event. It's layered, and each new loss can trigger unexpected depths of emotion. For me, this was a completely new level of grief.

Whenever the screen showed my wedding photo, me holding the sign "Forever your little girl," tears would flood my eyes. And when the video played "Thank God" by Kane and Katelyn Brown, it always stopped me. My mom had told me that was their song. Dad had once told her, with so much love, "I thank God for all these years with you."

The flood of feelings wasn't just emotional; it took a physical toll. My shoulders ached, and I barely slept. The longer I worked on the video, the more it brought back a flood of memories. Seeing Dad holding Mom's hand in nearly every photo reminded me just how deep their love ran. And every time I reached those moments, I felt like I was saying goodbye all over again.

Even as the days passed, loneliness became a new weight for Mom to carry.

MOM'S REFLECTIONS ON LONELINESS

Mom's Journal Entry – Friday 12/09/22

"Today is Friday. Today we are working on the garage. My son is so helpful.

I'm already thinking of him leaving. Wish he was closer to me. I miss him so much when he leaves me.

Why are we not closer to each other? He means so much, all the calls he makes to me every night. It keeps me going."

Mom's Journal Entry – Saturday 12/10/22

"Today is Saturday. My son left today. After having him for a week and then having him leave is scary!

I've never been alone; dad was always here. He always protected me and was always a great partner. We talked and laughed a lot. It was always so easy. Marriage was always easy with him.

I will be alone for the first time!"

Mom's Journal Entry – Sunday 12/11/22

"I feel like every time I turn around, I am crying. Took the all the bedding and washed everything. After I went to make the bed, and I just laid on it and cried. He always helped me make the bed.

I cried so hard!

I just feel that it should get better, but it doesn't ... after a day that was so sad I picked up a card.

My youngest son came home with dinner. I love it when he hugs me. He has my husband's hugs. Thank the Lord for him being here.

I just couldn't have been alone right now. ☹ *"*

In the darkest stretches, even the smallest gestures can offer a lifeline. We knew we couldn't take away her sorrow, but we hoped we could give her something she could turn to on the hardest days. After Dad passed, my husband and I sent Mom a jar of KindNotes—a collection of tiny, sealed messages filled with encouragement and hope. She decided to open them only on days she needed a boost, eventually taping each note/card into her journal. On this day the KindNotes she pulled said, "**I will miss you every day until I see you again.**"

Mom's Journal Entry – Wednesday 12/14/22

"Today is Wednesday. I think about how I miss that warm hug in the morning. It was great! It doesn't seem to be getting better yet. I just want to breathe. I went out for lunch with my son. Not much of an appetite. He left and I went to Target. Thought maybe if I walked around it might be good for me. It wasn't ... I cried through the whole store. I finally left for home. This is the only place I feel safe.

How stupid is that ... What do I do with the rest of my life? I'm trying to look toward my future. I really am."

Mom's Journal Entry – Thursday 12/15/22

"I spent the day talking and telling others that my loving husband was gone. I cried and cried and cried ... I'm still in disbelief.

Friends came over and brought me pizza and we just talked. I just realized I'm a widow. Never thought I'd say that. I feel like I'm on repeat mode.

I wonder what my life will be like going forward.

Forward is a strange word right now. I look forward to leaving to go see family next week for Christmas. I know I'll miss him on the drive."

Mom's Journal Entry – Saturday 12/17/22

"Today I spent the day calling several people. It was mentally trying. It feels so nice to see how many people adored him and said he was an amazing person. I knew that but it was so nice to hear it. I was so blessed to have such a wonderful person as my partner in life. It makes me so sad to go on without him. ☹"

THE START OF LIFE AFTER | 55

Mom's Journal Entry – Tuesday 12/20/22

"LJ and I went to Mesa to get dad. So sad ☹ Just want to say it's over and he's coming home. Got the death certificates and they said lung cancer. It said for years. How can that be??? He never complained! Did he keep the pain from me? I just don't understand.

Today I found out I'm probably going to have surgery. Go figure and have kidney stones again. Crap!!! Why me?

Everything seems like a struggle! Time for a love note …

 "

The KindNotes mom pulled said, "**We never lose the people we love. They live with us in our hearts for the rest of our lives.**"

Mom's Journal Entry – Wednesday 12/21/22

"LJ and I went to dinner to celebrate Christmas together. We went to Olive Garden. He gave me a 4-leaf clover necklace and we put it in the necklace. He said he went to the funeral home to buy it.

He crushed up the 50-year-old four leaf clover and put it in it, instead of ashes. What a nice surprise! That's probably the most sincere gesture that he has ever done.

I am a little scared to leave tomorrow alone, but I have to start somewhere, by myself. Miss packing for me and dad. Feel a little lost."

Mom's Journal Entry – Christmas day 12/25/22

"<u>Christmas day</u>.

It was a lonely day without my love! <u>But</u> the children made it special, and I got through the day. I could <u>NEVER</u> have been able to do it without <u>all</u> of them. <u>God how I miss him</u>! His hugs were the best. We fit perfectly together. He was always so soft and warm. I <u>always</u> knew he loved me. Now that's over I need to put my best foot forward and march on to a new life without him. I wonder what next year will have for me? Merry Christmas babe. ♥"

Mom's Journal Entry – Monday 12/26/22

"I spent the day with Anthony's family. They are so nice. ♥ I wish I lived closer to Laura. She and I get along so well.

Tammy cooked prime rib. Boy was it good!!!

Told Frank and Laura what happened. Sometimes when I tell the story it makes me feel like his life was worth talking about. Tomorrow, I leave."

Mom's Journal Entry – Thursday 12/29/22

"Today is Thursday.

Today has been 1 month since I lost my husband.

It all seems like a blur ... I'm still sick! He would always care for me.

He was the best! I really miss him.

It's nana birthday today. I'm sure she is I heaven with him. I believe she came and got him when C. saw her."

Her KindNotes said, "**I love myself as I am.**"

As the holidays faded and a new year began, Mom's tone shifted subtly. Her reflections became less about surviving the day and more about imagining how she might carry herself forward. This next entry marked that emotional pivot.

Mom's Journal Entry – 01/01/23

"A new year and I am going to live alone, <u>NOT</u> be alone.

Am I healing or is it just a moment in time during the process?"

Mom's Journal Entry – Thursday 1/5/23

"Talked to Tammy yesterday and she cried so hard. My heart hurts for her. I can remember every time she would call, she would say, 'Tell dad I love him,' and he would smile so big and say, 'I love her too.' I know how she feels and it's an awful heart ache!"

DREAM VISITATIONS AND NEXT STEPS

By February, I was still crying myself to sleep most nights, emotionally and physically drained from it all. Then one night, I had a dream, though it felt like more than just a dream. I was sitting with Mom, recalling all the lessons Dad had taught me: how to stand on my own two feet, how to never settle, how to change a tire in case I was ever stuck alone on the road—something I've had to do more than once. In the dream, Dad rose from his bed and walked over to me. He gently placed his hand on my arm. I could feel its warmth, as real as if he were still beside me. He told me he wasn't in pain. He reminded me how proud he was and how deeply he loved me. Then, just as suddenly, a young child stood next to him and then he was gone.

I woke up in tears and looked at the clock. It read 4:45 a.m., the same time he had passed. I wrote down every detail before I could forget. Later, I learned this was known as a visitation dream: a vivid encounter where you feel an intense connection with a loved one who has passed. These dreams often carry with them a deep sense of peace and unexpected comfort. For me, that moment offered a kind of quiet closure I hadn't even known I was still longing for. I felt wrapped in warmth and gratitude and I'm especially thankful I took the time to write down every detail I could remember.

UNDERSTANDING THE STAGES OF GRIEF

Before we move forward, let's revisit the seven stages of grief: shock, denial, anger, bargaining, depression, testing, and acceptance. They aren't linear; you can bounce between them unpredictably. You might feel acceptance one day, only to slip into anger or despair the next. That's normal.

Grief is also intensely personal. You might feel guilty, as I did, wondering if you did all you could for your loved one. You might feel numb, disconnected, or helpless. And life truly doesn't revert to what it was. Part of grief is learning to exist in a new reality.

I remember seeing one of my brothers process his own sorrow—through anger. It was as though regret weighed on him, and I'll never forget when he sank to his knees, gripping Dad's hand after he passed, while tears of heartbreak and remorse poured from him. Remember, it's OK to cry, to talk about your loved one, and to seek support.

EXERCISE: REFLECTING ON YOUR GRIEF JOURNEY

If you find yourself in a place of uncertainty, consider trying the following:

1. **Find a Quiet Space**: Take a few minutes to sit with your thoughts. This might be a place that feels safe or comforting to you—at home, in nature, or even in your car.
2. **Journal Prompt**: Write about a memory with your loved one. It could be something joyful, something you miss, or even something difficult. Focus on the emotions that memory brings up.
3. **Identify Your Stage**: Ask yourself which stage(s) of grief you're in. Denial? Anger? Acceptance? You might find yourself in more than one.
4. **Give Yourself Permission**: Whatever you feel, it's OK. Jot down one small action you can take to honor your loved one or care for yourself.

This isn't something you "get over." It becomes part of who you are. Writing can help you see your progress and remind you of how far you've come, even when it seems impossible. Even two years after my dad's passing, tears still come when I talk about the beautiful impact he had on our lives. It's not the gut-wrenching sob of the early days, but a deep ache that reminds me of his absence.

Life moves forward, even as sorrow continues to linger. My oldest child recently got married and is now expecting their first baby, my first grandchild. I vividly remember how radiant my dad's joy was when I shared the news of my first baby. Now, as that grandchild prepares to complete the circle of life, I feel a nostalgic mix of excitement and sorrow. Every milestone reminds me of Dad's enduring love and the legacy he left behind, shaping our lives with both joy and remembrance.

Adjusting to a new reality takes time. Give yourself permission to take all the time you need. Grief never truly ends, but neither does love.

Date

What memories or emotions are resurfacing today?

What memories or emotions are resurfacing today?

I thought reaching this point meant the hardest part was behind me. But grief doesn't follow a timeline. It lingers in unexpected ways, sometimes loud, sometimes quiet.

As I took my first unsteady steps into life after losing Dad, I discovered something unexpected—not just more sorrow, but also quiet energy and surprising hints of hope, patiently waiting around the corner.

What memories or emotions are resurfacing today?

CHAPTER SIX

THE IMPACT OF PAST GRIEF

When I lost my Dad, grief hit me harder than anything I had ever experienced. It wasn't like the heartache I felt when I lost my grandparents or other loved ones; this was Dad. He helped shape my life, side by side with Mom. The weight of his absence felt deeply personal. Yet as I navigated my own sorrow, I couldn't help but think about my husband and the old wounds Dad's passing might have opened in him.

Years ago, in his early twenties, my husband lost his mom to breast cancer. Losing a parent so young leaves lasting scars, and I knew Dad's death could stir up memories he hadn't fully processed. He had been close to Dad, too, and I worried that this fresh loss would reawaken grief from his mom's passing.

I noticed it one afternoon while we were sitting on the bed. The sun was low, casting that familiar golden light across the room. My husband sat quietly, holding his phone, barely even looking at it. His gaze was fixed on nothing in particular, but I could see it, his eyes were distant, like he wasn't really with me.

"I've been thinking about my mom a lot lately," he said, barely above a whisper.

That's when I knew, Dad's passing had cracked open something he'd long kept sealed. He'd spoken about her before, but this was different. Thoughts of her, her laugh, her fight against cancer, her absence during all of life's big events, were flooding back. He admitted that after she died, he spent more than a year hiding his grief from everyone, even from his dad. Life had moved forward so quickly, and he'd buried that pain deep to keep going.

Now, that sorrow was rising again. It wasn't just about losing my dad; it was about the anticipation of one day losing his. His rock. His constant.

We sat there in silence, the kind that doesn't need words. I reached over and held his hand. For once, I wasn't the only one falling apart. And somehow, in that shared sorrow, we both felt a little less alone.

It was a delicate balance: trying to be there for him while also supporting my mom, my family, and myself.

Grief has a way of stacking itself upon itself. Each new loss can reactivate the pain of previous ones, a phenomenon often called **compounded grief or layered grief**. In our case, as I grieved for Dad, I saw my husband struggle with sadness, anger, and helplessness tied to his mom's death. It felt like a wave pulling him back into old emotions, magnifying the intensity of our current heartache. We weren't just grieving Dad; we were also reliving the passing of his mom. Sometimes, it seemed like the weight of our combined sorrows was more than either of us could bear.

The complexity of compounded grief can be startling. You find yourself mourning both the old and the new, with emotions piling up like layers you can't separate. Certain dates, anniversaries, birthdays, holiday memories, or even scents might trigger vivid flashbacks to previous losses, making the present feel even heavier. It's exhausting, like an emotional cycle you can't break free from, as you are in the center of it all. I noticed that I started coping differently this time. I was learning that some past experiences with death had built up my resilience: I understood my husband's fight through his mom's death, and I learned from his strength. When I lost my grandparents, I learned that understanding emotion means embracing both the profound sorrow of death and the warmth of cherished memories. For instance, I recall playing in the yard as a kid, running into the house and grabbing a cookie, handed to me by my smiling nana. Surrounded by family and the lingering scent of home-cooked meals, I learned that every tear was interlaced with a bittersweet reminder of our joyful times together. I remember when my papa died. I saw his urn on the mantle and wondered why nana had it there and why he had to leave us. I didn't fully understand my feelings until after my dad passed away, when I realized that holding on to his memory brings us comfort.

When I think back, I remember being surprised by how deeply my husband and I felt at once, two monumental losses intertwined, and it was hard to know where one ended and the other began. Yet the lingering pain from that earlier death also challenged his ability to process Dad's passing in the present. At times, we balanced it gracefully; at other times, we stumbled. I was grateful for my husband's fortitude, though. While I worried he might be overwhelmed by revisiting his mom's death, he allowed himself to feel the emotions without letting them consume him. In a way, watching him handle both losses reminded me that grief can change you without defining you.

UNDERSTANDING COMPOUNDED GRIEF

It took me a while to realize that grief can compound over time, stirring old hurts with each new loss, a layered effect that still catches me off guard. If you've lost someone close in the past, a fresh loss might bring back unresolved emotions or guilt. Some people find it an opportunity to heal old wounds; for others, it's like being catapulted back into a storm they thought had passed. I saw echoes of that in my brother, too. His unresolved emotions resurfaced when Dad died, adding another layer of hurt to an already devastating experience.

Old grief can sneak up on you: a familiar place, a specific smell, or a cherished keepsake might trigger vivid recollections. You might feel guilty for dwelling on an earlier loss while facing a new one. But it's a normal part of grief. Each heartbreak leaves a mark, and when they layer, the weight can be enormous. Recognizing that all your reactions, both past and present, are valid is crucial. There's no right way to grieve, and it's important to honor the complexity of your emotions.

EXERCISE: UNPACKING LAYERED GRIEF

If you're coping with grief from both past and present losses, these reflections may help you find clarity and begin to heal. The following exercise is designed to help you explore how past grief affects your current experience and to guide you through the process of acknowledgment and rebuilding.

1. **Reflect on a Previous Loss:** Think about an important past loss. It could be a loved one, a pet, or a major life shift. How did that affect you at the time? Write down any emotions, memories, or regrets that arise.

2. **Acknowledge How It's Reappearing:** Notice how that previous grief is resurfacing now. Are you sensing familiar feelings—sadness, anger, guilt—tied to your current loss? Identify any triggers that bring back those old emotions.

3. **Identify Past Coping Strategies:** Recall what helped you cope before. Did talking with someone ease your pain? Did writing or having a creative outlet offer comfort? Write

down those strategies that worked in the past; they might help again now.

4. **Create a Plan for Moving Forward:** Grieving in layers means honoring both old and new losses. Consider how you can memorialize those you've lost or channel your emotions productively, through your writing, therapy, or sharing stories with supportive friends and family.

5. **Be Gentle with Yourself:** Finally, give yourself permission to feel it all. Grief is messy, and experiencing multiple layers at once can be overwhelming. Healing takes time, and you're allowed to move at your own pace.

Coping with compounded grief is never easy. But by acknowledging old losses and understanding how they intensify today's sorrow, you can heal in a way that honors both the people you've lost and the person you are becoming. This chapter is a reminder that while grief may be layered, your capacity for strength is layered too. You carry both sorrow and resilience forward as you continue your path.

Date

Compounded sorrow taught me that loss doesn't erase love; it stretches it. It reminds you that the people who shaped you are never really gone. They live in your memories, your stories, and the quiet way you carry forward. In grieving them, we also grow. Layer by layer, we become more whole, not in spite of the discomfort, but because of it.

CHAPTER SEVEN

THE EMOTION OF IT ALL

Grief comes in unexpected surges. Sometimes it crashes into you; other times it drifts in quietly, pulling at your heart. Over the past two years, I've experienced more than my fair share of these waves, but it wasn't just my emotions I felt I had to manage; it was everyone else's, too. My mom was heartbroken in a way I had never witnessed before, my siblings were dealing with their worries, and emotions, and friends kept reaching out, each person needing reassurance we were OK or wanting to be a listening ear. I often found myself swallowing my own sadness so I could comfort them first. That sense of responsibility, to hold it together for everyone else, only magnified my own grief, leaving me wondering if I'd ever have the space to process my own pain.

RESPECTING EVERYONE'S GRIEF

Grief rarely happens in isolation; its effects ripple out to the people closest to us in ways we often don't anticipate. My brothers, my mom, and my husband each faced Dad's passing in a deeply personal manner, and I discovered how crucial it was to respect each of their grieving styles, even when it wasn't easy. Their emotions became just as significant as my own in our collective journey toward rebuilding.

The day Dad passed away, the look of shock on my younger brother's face said it all. It hit him like a freight train. Part of me wondered if he had been in denial about how sick Dad was, which made the reality so much harder for him to accept. I felt frustrated, thinking, "Why didn't you talk to Dad before it was too late?" I had encouraged him countless times to share those final conversations. When it didn't happen, I felt angry, not at him as a person, but at the missed opportunity for closure.

With my older brother, the dynamic was different. I craved a deep conversation with him, something that could help both of us heal, but he kept his feelings mostly locked away. His priority was caring for Mom and making sure she was OK. We had only one serious talk about Dad's death, and in that fleeting moment, I glimpsed the raw pain he tried so hard to hide. Even that brief encounter made it clear just how deeply he loved Dad.

My husband concerned me in a different way; he still needed me to remember myself, the person he fell in love with. I recognized some of the emotions I was wrestling with, even if I couldn't fully process them. In trying to handle everything and support those around me, I overlooked how sometimes he just wanted to chat about anything else. He wanted to give me a break from the constant weight of it all.

He navigated this personal what I would call my "minefield" with a grace that left me in awe, instinctively knowing when I needed a so-called break long before I did. I didn't even realize I needed those moments. I don't know how he found such balance, but I'll forever be grateful for him just listening and having simple talks about the day or our kids.

Then there was Mom. Her range of emotions stretched from incredible sadness to palpable fear. My biggest worry was that she might succumb to heartbreak, given how inseparable she and Dad had been. She tried to be strong for everyone else, but I knew she was fighting an internal battle. I can still hear the tremor in her voice when she once said, "Your father visited you and your brothers in dreams, but not me. Why?" The pain in her words was so real; she longed for any hint of connection with him.

THE IMPACT OF GRIEF ON CHILDREN

While my own grief felt overwhelming, I wasn't prepared for how Dad's death would affect my children. They lost their papa, but they also had to watch me bear my raw emotions day after day. Each of them reacted differently: One appeared to handle it with surprising maturity, another tried to nurture me, and my third child began struggling in school. I can't say for certain it was entirely due to Dad's passing, but it happened close enough to raise a red flag. That's when I realized how vital it is to remain aware of children's emotional health during times of loss.

Grief hits children in unique ways, shaped by age, personality, and emotional resilience. Younger kids might not grasp the permanence of death, while older ones might bottle up their emotions or express them through anger or withdrawal. Each child's response is valid, and as parents or caregivers, we owe it to them to tailor our support to their needs. Here are some strategies that may help:

WAYS TO HELP A CHILD COPE WITH GRIEF

1. **Open Communication:** Encourage kids to talk about their feelings and ask questions. Use straightforward, honest language—phrases like "gone to sleep" can confuse them about the finality of death.

2. **Validate Their Emotions:** Assure children it's OK to feel sad, angry, scared, or even relieved. Let them know their emotions are normal and acceptable.

3. **Maintain Routine:** Keep daily schedules as consistent as possible. Familiar routines provide stability when life feels out of control.

4. **Offer Comfort:** Be present, physically and emotionally. A hug, a calm tone of voice, or simply sitting with them can be incredibly reassuring.

5. **Model Healthy Grieving:** Let them see you cry or talk about your loved one. This normalizes the grieving process, teaching children that sadness and healing can coexist.

6. **Use Creative Outlets:** Encourage drawing, journaling, or other forms of expression. These activities can help kids articulate complex emotions they might not be able to name yet.

7. **Provide Age-Appropriate Resources:** Books, videos, or activities geared toward children can help them understand and cope with loss. Check libraries or online platforms for suggestions.

8. **Seek Professional Support:** If a child's grief substantially disrupts their life—behavioral changes, academic issues, withdrawn behavior—consider a child therapist specializing in grief.

ADDITIONAL TIPS FOR GRIEVING TOGETHER

- **Create Rituals:** Light a candle, share favorite stories, or do an activity your loved one enjoyed; invite children to participate.
- **Listen Actively:** Sometimes kids just want to be heard, not "fixed." Give them space to speak without judgment.
- **Observe Behavioral Changes:** Keep an eye on sleeping, eating, or academic shifts, as these often signal deeper struggles.

By being attuned to their needs, you can help children form healthy coping skills and resilience. Grieving as a family can strengthen your bonds, too, creating shared moments of recovery. But remember, you know your child best. While these tips can guide you, trust your instincts when it comes to supporting them.

Returning to Mom's reflections, she once told me she had prayed for help when Dad's Alzheimer's was getting worse. When the stage 4 lung cancer diagnosis came, she tried to view it as a sort of silver lining; Dad's Alzheimer's shielded him from fully realizing how dire his cancer was. It was a difficult perspective, but in her mind, it eased some of her anguish. In her journal, she wrote:

Mom's Journal Entry – Sunday 1/22/23

"The last 2 days have been horrible. I cried a lot. Just feel so lost without him. Just wonder if I can make it. I'm trying but don't feel like I'm making head way at all. Where do I go from here? None of it makes sense.

I tell myself there are lots of people in the world who lose someone special. They make it, so why not me? I don't want to eat, take a shower, get dressed, wear makeup. I just keep trying.

I keep waiting for the day that seems worthwhile. I just don't know. I miss him so much, it hurts. I opened this card and it told me, 'Get up in the morning and tell yourself I CAN DO THIS.' Hope so!"

My own healing was hard enough, but trying to honor everyone else's made it more complicated. I had to break down each relationship—my brothers, my husband, my mom—and figure out how their emotions affected me. Only after sorting through those layers could I fully move forward myself. The anger I felt surprised me. Some people in our circle were furious at the doctors, blaming them for not doing more. I didn't share that anger, but I did harbor resentment toward my brothers for not speaking at Dad's celebration of life. "How could they stay silent?" I wondered. Dad adored them; why wouldn't they say something?

Pouring my energy into creating a tribute video became my way of expressing both my gratitude and my sorrow. Hunting for old photos and memories was like rediscovering hidden treasures of Dad's life. And on the day of the celebration, I mustered the energy to give a short speech. My mother-in-law stood by me as I spoke, and her quiet support kept me steady.

Over time, I realized it wasn't about what people did or didn't say. I didn't need my brothers to speak to know they were grieving in their own way. As I healed, I let go of the resentment. Their presence was enough. This can be a hard place to put ourselves, as we want to comfort and help them process this grief. But in the end it is up to them to process it.

Grief appears in many countless ways; shock, tears, anger, guilt, and even occasional moments of peace. Observing how my family managed those varied emotions taught me that grief is deeply personal. I've learned that not everyone is ready to show their feelings publicly, and that's OK. I've learned to respect how each person grieves in their own way.

EXERCISE: UNDERSTANDING THE EMOTIONAL LAYERS OF GRIEF

Everyone grieves differently. Some people openly share their emotions, while others turn inward. This exercise is designed to help you explore your own feelings and acknowledge the emotions of those around you.

1. **Identify Your Emotions**

Begin by writing down how you feel today. What surfaces when you think of your loved one—anger, sadness, relief, confusion? Then dig deeper: Why do you feel this way? For example, "I feel anger because I wish the doctors had done more," or "I feel peace because they're no longer suffering."

2. **Observe Others**

Consider the people closest to you. What are they showing or not showing about their heartache? How does their emotional response affect you? Do you feel comforted, confused, or frustrated? Write down these observations.

3. **Communicate with Compassion**

Create a list of those with whom you would like to speak. Pick one person from your list and reach out to them. It doesn't have to be a big gesture. A simple note, a shared memory, or a moment of quiet together can bridge emotional distance. This act of compassion can help you both understand the importance of feelings and feeling seen.

4. **Release Expectations**

Reflect on any assumptions you're holding about how others "should" grieve. Let them go. Remember that everyone's journey looks different.

By acknowledging your own emotions and the emotions of those around you, you can move through the many layers with greater empathy. Grief can feel isolating but it's not a solitary experience. We're all in it together, even if each of us takes our own path.

Date

I thought I'd finally learned to ride the waves of emotion that came with losing Dad. Grief doesn't end; it changes shape. As I continued to walk through my own mourning, I found deeper compassion for the people beside me, and for the tender, complex emotions we all carry.

CHAPTER EIGHT

STEPPING FORWARD

Grief isn't about "getting over it"; it's about learning to carry love and loss hand in hand. The idea of "moving on" doesn't mean leaving grief behind; it means honoring the love, the memories, and even sadness in new ways. **Grief doesn't end; it evolves.** The journey is messy and nonlinear, a mix of doubt, fear, hope, and sometimes guilt. You might wonder, "**Is it OK to feel joy again? Am I betraying my loved one by continuing to live?**" These questions are natural, especially when you start shifting from mourning to living.

Mom's Journal Entry – Tuesday 2/14/23

"Today is Tuesday. Happy Valentine's Day! Miss you so much!!! Our son brought me flowers, so sweet. That meant so much to me. I love him. Your sister and I cried today. It *felt good to let it out to someone that is alone too. I love you, Babe Xoxo."*

She pulled a KindNotes that said, "**When someone you love becomes a memory, the memory becomes a treasure.**" —Unknown author.

Mom's Journal Entry – Wednesday 2/15/23

"Karen and I packed up for the trip to Vegas this week! We spent the day shopping and talking about our lives and how we both lost our husbands. How we, can't believe it."

We had Dad's celebration of life on February 18, 2023. We used Mom's journal as a guest book so she could have the names and comments of everyone who joined us. She pulled a KindNotes at the end of the day that said, "**Although it's difficult today to see beyond the sorrow. May looking back in memory help comfort you tomorrow.**"

For me, stepping forward after Dad's death was like learning to walk on unfamiliar ground. I had to rebuild parts of myself while still clinging to the person I was before he passed. I wasn't even sure what "forward" meant at first. Did it mean getting through a day without breaking down? Making plans for the future without feeling something was missing?

Eventually, I realized that moving forward didn't mean forgetting Dad or letting everything go; it meant weaving the loss into my life while allowing myself room to thrive. It meant feeling joy without guilt, sadness without despair, and hope without fear. That's when I began to see that living with grief wasn't just about merely surviving. It's about embracing life's richness even as sorrow remains a part of it.

EVOLVING GRIEF

One of the hardest lessons was understanding that grief can come and go like waves. Some days I felt capable, as if the weight of loss had lifted. On other days, the smallest reminder would bring it all back. Grief became a constant, sometimes just a background presence that surfaced at milestones, holidays, birthdays, or even routine tasks when I would've asked Dad for advice. Decorating for Halloween, for example, always reminded me of how he carved the best pumpkins, a tradition he passed on to all my children. At first, these memories were tinged with sadness, but over time, I learned to cherish them. They became tokens of the love he left behind, and honoring these traditions felt like keeping his spirit alive.

Mom's Journal Entry – Friday 3/10/23

"Happy Anniversary I LOVE YOU, well we almost made it. 50 years and he was so proud of that. I am so glad we celebrated in October with everyone. All he ever wanted was to be with all 3 kids together. He got his wish.

When I think back it worked out beautifully. Some people never get that opportunity to be together at the end and have 50 years together even though it never seems enough.

I love you babe 'A bushel and a peck and hug around the neck' as you would always say to me at night when we went to bed.

Happy Anniversary My Love.

XOXO."

(Mom pulled a KindNotes that simply said, "**I love you, Mom.**")

Mom's Journal Entry – Monday 4/24/23

"Today is Monday. It's now almost 5 months. It seems like yesterday. I wonder if he came back just one more time. (she expressed if she could have done something different)

I remember back to being in the lobby at the hotel in San Diego. I remember thinking he doesn't look good at all. Thinking he's getting worse. But I think I still didn't get it.

I'm mad at myself for not realizing what's REALLY happening. I'm mad I didn't hold him at night."

The KindNotes this time said, "**Smile at the memories that are all around you.**"

Mom's Journal Entry – Wednesday 04/26/23

"Today my son and I went to McDonald's to have lunch. After ordering lunch, I explained to my son that this was the last place Dad was, before he went to the hospital. Then I said, 'What's our number for lunch?' Then we both looked, and we were shocked about the number! (747) That was Dad's favorite airplane. It was as if he was there with us. Oh, how I miss him. It is still unbelievable to me."

(Mom taped the McDonald's receipt into her book.)

HONORING TRADITIONS

Stepping forward doesn't mean letting go. It means continuing to live and holding on to the love and lessons our loved ones gave us. It's OK to laugh, to feel happiness, and to create new memories while still treasuring the old ones. Sometimes, grief resurfaces unexpectedly, and that's all right; that's simply proof of the enduring love.

EMBRACING JOY WITHOUT GUILT

These days, holidays are bittersweet. I'm more grateful for small things, like those Coca-Cola ornaments Dad adored. Hanging them on the tree each year feels like having him right there with us. I watch Mom too. After over fifty years of careful holiday decorating, she once considered stopping altogether after losing Dad. "Why bother? It's not the same," she'd say. But in time, she returned to decorating and that simple act comforts me and my family. It reminds me that resilience is possible and that honoring what was once shared can help us heal.

Ultimately, stepping forward means integrating grief into our lives, not as something to fix or discard, but as part of us that coexists with joy, hope, and love all at once. Grief may never disappear entirely, but that doesn't stop us from living fully. Through this process, we become stronger, more compassionate, and more connected to those around us.

EXERCISE: LEARNING TO CARRY GRIEF

Stepping forward isn't about leaving grief behind; it's about living alongside it while embracing new possibilities. Use this exercise to reflect on carrying your grief in a way that honors your loved one and lets you move forward.

1. **Acknowledge Grief's Presence**:
   The ways grief surfaces in your life. Are certain dates, places, or activities more triggering? Recognizing these patterns is the first way to begin navigating them.
2. **Embrace Meaningful Memories**:

Think of a memory that makes you smile when you recall your loved one. Write it down. Notice how it can bring both joy and sadness. Allow both emotions to coexist without judgment.

3. **Create a New Tradition:**
Consider ways to honor your loved one's memory, an annual ritual, a simple act of remembrance, or a personal tribute. Incorporating them into your life in small yet powerful ways can help you move forward.

4. **Release Guilt, Accept Joy:**
Reflect on any guilt you feel about experiencing happiness again. Write down affirmations or reasons why it's OK to find joy, even in grief. Joy does not negate love or the loss; it can coexist alongside them.

5. **Reflect on Your Growth:**
Look back on your grief journey. How have you grown? What insights have you gained about love, life, or yourself? Recognize the courage it took to reach this point, however uneven or slow the path may be.

By accepting that stepping forward means integrating both loss and love, we learn to live fully, even as grief remains a part of us.

Date

Reflections from Chapter Eight – Stepping Forward with Grief

I took a tentative step toward rebuilding my life, only to discover that letting go was far more complicated than I'd imagined. What I believed was steady ground would soon shift beneath my feet again, challenging every bit of strength I'd come to rely on.

CHAPTER NINE

WHAT TO REMEMBER

As we near the end of this book, my hope is that these words have offered you comfort, insight, and perhaps a sense of companionship through the complex terrain of grief. While it is deeply personal, there are universal truths that can guide us. The lessons you take away might differ from my own, but I encourage you to keep stepping toward healing, adapting these insights to your own unique path.

Below are the key lessons I've learned, guiding principles that I hope you'll carry with you:

1. **Understanding the Unseen Change**: I once spoke of "change we never saw coming." That subtle yet profound shift that occurs when someone we love is no longer here. This change isn't only external; it transforms us internally. Our view of the world, ourselves, and our future is forever altered. Life doesn't pause for grief. Instead, it becomes part of life's ongoing rhythm, shaping us in ways we might not immediately recognize.

What to remember: Grief is a transformation, not a single moment in time. It changes you, but it doesn't have to diminish you.

Date

Your grief has a voice—let these pages hold it for you

2. **Respecting the Grief of Others:** Grief sends ripples outward, affecting everyone around us. Family, friends, and loved ones process loss in their own ways. Whether it's your siblings, parents, or partner, respecting these unique responses is essential.

What to remember: Everyone grieves differently. Be patient with yourself and others. Grief is shared, even when it looks different for each person.

Date

2. **Holding Space for Complexity:** One of the hardest aspects of grief is making room for conflicting emotions. You might feel peace and sorrow, or relief and longing, all at once. Throughout this book, we discussed the duality of grief: joy and sadness, anger and acceptance, pain and love. Healing looks different for each of us—be it family, friends, or ourselves. Some people speak openly, while others remain silent. Releasing expectations of how grief "should" look can relieve unnecessary pressure.

Your grief has a voice—let these pages hold it for you

Self-compassion is essential. You'll have moments of doubt, frustration, and guilt. You may wonder whether you're grieving "the right way." Remember, there is no perfect way to grieve.

What to remember: You're allowed to feel conflicting emotions. Healing doesn't follow a straight path. Be gentle with yourself.

Date

4. The Power of Connection and Communication:

We explored how crucial it is to communicate, whether sharing memories or simply being there for one another. Grief can isolate us, but connection is key to healing. Reaching out, even in small ways, helps both you and the people grieving alongside you. Support often exists if you seek it, through family, friends, or professional resources.

What to remember: Don't be afraid to reach out. Connection and communication can be deeply therapeutic, even when words come slowly.

WHAT TO REMEMBER

Date

5. Spiritual Signs and Dream Visitations:

We discussed the sense of comfort that can arise from dream visitations or spiritual experiences. Whether you see these as literal or symbolic, they can help bridge the gap between loss and memory. Many find peace in these moments, feeling a continued connection to those who've passed. I suggest keeping track of these special moments, whether by writing them down, as I did, or recording them verbally. This way you can revisit them whenever you need. They're the kind of experiences you'll definitely want to remember.

What to remember: Stay open to the ways loved ones may continue connecting with you—through dreams, memories, or the lasting impact they had on your life.

Date
___

6. **Carrying Forward Traditions and Memories**: A powerful way to honor someone who has passed is to carry on their traditions, holiday customs, hobbies, or the small rituals. These practices not only honor their legacy but also offer strength and warmth in the present. By preserving what your loved one cherished, you allow their legacy to live on.

What to remember: Moving forward doesn't mean leaving your loved one behind. You carry them with you by continuing the traditions and values they held dear.

WHAT TO REMEMBER | 104

Date

7. **The Layered Process of Healing**: Healing from grief isn't a straight line. You'll face setbacks—days when the pain feels as fresh and devastating as ever. But over time, you may find greater depth in your memories, and moments of peace gradually start to outnumber the moments of sorrow.

What to remember: Healing takes time and unfolds in layers. Allow yourself the grace and space to heal at your own pace.

Date
_____
_____
_____
_____
_____
_____
_____
_____
_____
_____
_____
_____
_____

8. Stepping Forward with Hope

Finally, stepping forward is not about forgetting your loss; it's about integrating it into your life and finding a way to live fully again. It means acknowledging the discomfort while also making room for hope and joy.

What to remember: It's not about getting over a loss. It's about learning to live with it and permitting yourself to feel happiness without guilt.

Date

WHAT TO REMEMBER

RESOURCES FOR SUPPORT

Grief can be overwhelming. While this book offers guidance, sometimes additional support may be essential. Here are some resources that shaped this book and might support you on your own journey:

GRIEF SUPPORT GROUPS

- **Grief Share:** A national network of support groups for those coping with loss. griefshare.org
- **The Compassionate Friends:** Support for families grieving the loss of a child. compassionatefriends.org
- **Modern Loss:** Online community featuring articles, personal stories, and resources. modernloss.com

ONLINE RESOURCES AND ARTICLES

- **Psychology Today's Grief Resources:** Articles and tips for coping. psychologytoday.com
- **Help Guide's Coping with Grief and Loss:** Practical advice and strategies. helpguide.org

THERAPY AND COUNSELING

- **National Suicide Prevention Lifeline:** For immediate support with overwhelming grief. 1-800-273-8255, suicidepreventionlifeline.org
- **Better Help:** Online counseling sessions with licensed therapists. betterhelp.com

JOURNALING AND PERSONAL REFLECTION

Writing your thoughts and feelings can bring clarity. Consider prompts like:

1. "What are three memories of my loved one that bring me comfort?"

2. "How have I seen myself grow through this grief journey?"
3. "What would I like to say to my loved one today?"

I believe deeply in the power of journaling and writing your thoughts down. At the end of this book, you'll find a section dedicated to helping you continue these reflections. We'll explore that section more shortly.

PERSONAL REFLECTIONS

Grief isn't something you "finish" or "get over." It's a part of you that evolves over time. Sharing my lessons and stories has been a crucial part of my transformation, and I hope it has offered you solace. My experiences with loss have shown me the importance of self-compassion, connection, and remembrance. Through writing, I honor the love that endures, and I continue stepping forward. I hope you can do the same in your own time and in your own way.

I once believed I'd gathered all the lessons grief had to teach me, but I realized there was still one more piece to explore; an invitation to look inward and let your own story guide you to a deeper understanding.

CHAPTER TEN

THE POWER OF JOURNALING

I believe that reflection is an essential part of healing. Throughout this book, you've read about the complexities of grief, the duality of emotions, the challenge of carrying forward memories and traditions, and the delicate balance between sorrow and joy. Yet your journey doesn't end here. Writing down your thoughts, emotions, and memories can provide clarity and peace as you continue to heal.

Journaling offers a personal space to explore your feelings, track your growth, and reconnect with the memories of your loved ones. By recording both sorrow and joy, you make room for both as you move forward. That's why I've included a journaling section at the end of this book—to encourage you to continue reflecting long after you've turned the final page.

Take your time. There is no rush to heal, and there is no "right way" to process everything. Use the prompts provided or write freely. Let this be your space to honor memories, to explore your emotions, and ultimately to find your path toward rebuilding. As I navigate sadness in my own life and prepare for the future, especially as we face the news of new loved ones battling cancer, I have come to understand that grief isn't the conclusion of the story; it's an integral part of the journey.

Thank you for taking the time to read this book and for looking closely at my own grief as well as my mom's. As you begin (or continue) your own exercises, remember that becoming more comfortable with the discomfort of grief is already a meaningful step.

Grief isn't the conclusion of the story; it's an integral part of the journey.

PART 1 – AS DEATH APPROACHES

My story highlights how crucial it is to be organized before a loss occurs when possible. Even with the best preparation, we may still overlook things. We thought we were prepared for my dad's passing and the many decisions involved, but when the time came, everything happened quickly amid our vast emotions. Planning ahead can bring clarity and peace when you need it most.

This section is designed to help you, your loved ones, or anyone looking for guidance during such challenging times. While this list may not be exhaustive, it offers a strong starting point. Keep this information in a safe, secure location, and limit access to trusted individuals only.

LEGAL DOCUMENTS

1. **Will/Trust:** Ensure the will or trust is current and specify how assets will be distributed.

2. **Power of Attorney (POA):** Assign someone to make financial and legal decisions if you become incapacitated.

3. **Medical Power of Attorney:** Designate someone to make health care decisions on your behalf.

4. **Living Will/Advance Health Care Directive:** Outline your wishes for medical care, such as life support or resuscitation.

5. **Guardianship Papers:** If applicable, establish guardianship arrangements for minor children.

6. **Funeral and Burial Preferences:** Preplan or document preferences for funeral services, including the funeral home's contact information.

FINANCIAL DOCUMENTS

1. **Bank Accounts:** Keep account info accessible and consider joint accounts or payable on death (POD) designations. Remember, upon a loved one's death, financial institutions often freeze individual accounts.

2. **Insurance Policies:** Organize life, health, long-term care, and other insurance policies, including beneficiary information.

3. **Retirement Accounts:** Include details of IRAs, 401(k)s, pensions, and beneficiaries.

4. **Outstanding Debts:** Prepare a list of debts, loans, mortgages, and credit cards, to ease estate settlement.

5. **Social Security and Benefits:** Gather information on Social Security, pensions, or veteran benefits.

PROPERTY AND ASSETS

1. **Home and Property Titles:** Store deeds, titles, or ownership documents for all real estate together.

2. **Vehicle Titles:** Keep car and other vehicle titles in a secure place.

3. **Valuable Assets:** Inventory items like jewelry, artwork, and collectibles.

4. **Safe Deposit Box:** Provide keys, passwords, and a list of contents.

HEALTH AND MEDICAL INFORMATION

1. **Medications List:** Keep an updated list of current meds, doses, and health care providers.

2. **Health History:** Document past surgeries, chronic conditions, and allergies.

3. **Funeral Home Contact:** If you have a preferred funeral home, list the contact details here.

DIGITAL INFORMATION

1. **Digital Accounts**: Compile usernames, passwords, and access info for email, social media, and financial sites.

2. **Online Bill Pay Accounts:** Ensure someone can access online accounts to settle outstanding bills.

3. **Social Media Memorialization:** Platforms like Facebook and Instagram have memorial or legacy contact features. These allow users to set up options for account memorialization or designate someone to manage the account after they pass. This process may vary depending on the platform's policy, but they can provide you with guidance on memorialization preferences. This is important for ensuring you or a loved one's wishes are followed.

PERSONAL PREFERENCES

1. **Obituary Details:** Draft an obituary or key points you'd like included.

2. **Letters to Loved Ones:** If desired, write personal letters to be delivered after your passing.

3. **Personal Wishes for Final Days:** Note any requests for comfort or care near the end of life.

FINAL ARRANGEMENTS

1. **Funeral/Burial Prepayments:** If you've prearranged or prepaid, keep documentation organized.

2. **Charitable Contributions:** Specify any donations or memorial funds you'd like to establish.

3. **Body Donation:** If applicable, record your wish to donate your body for research or science.

IMPORTANT CONTACTS

Compile a list of key contacts, including family members and close friends. Remember to include medical providers, legal professionals, financial advisors, funeral services, insurance companies, the executor of your estate, and support groups or counselors. Also, keep notes on how to obtain multiple copies of death certificates for various legal and financial purposes:

- Family members and close friends
- Medical providers
- Legal professionals (attorney, estate planner)
- Financial advisors
- Funeral home or memorial services
- Insurance companies
- Executor of the estate
- Support groups or counselors

If these preparations feel daunting, remember you are not alone. As you step into the next section, I invite you to explore what's on your heart and mind with pen and paper, discovering the clarity that can come through reflection.

PART 2: JOURNAL – STARTING YOUR REFLECTION

Writing can be a powerful way to process emotions, find clarity, and honor cherished memories. This is where you can safely explore your thoughts, free from judgment or restriction. There are no right or wrong answers, only your truth.

Below are prompts to help you begin. Take your time with each one, allowing your emotions to unfold naturally. Write freely, without worrying about grammar or structure. If you ever feel stuck, return to these starters for inspiration:

REFLECTION PROMPTS

- What are three memories of my loved one that bring me comfort?
- How have I seen myself grow through this grief journey?
- What would I like to say to my loved one today?

If you're ready for a deeper exploration, consider these additional prompts:

1. What specific memories of my loved one bring me joy? How do these memories impact my grief journey?
2. Which emotions have surfaced since my loss? How do they influence my grief?

3. Who has helped me most? How have they eased my grief?
4. What insights about life or love have I gained? How do they shape my perspective now?
5. How might I honor my loved one in daily life—through rituals, traditions, or small acts?
6. What are my hopes and fears as I look to the future?
7. How can I be kinder to myself during grief? What affirmations do I need?
8. Which values or lessons from my loved one do I carry forward?
9. Recall a recent moment of happiness. How does it coexist with my sorrow?
10. What would I say in a letter to my loved one? What life updates or emotions would I share?

Date

UNTIL WE MEET AGAIN

As I close this chapter, I'm reminded of my early days of loss, feeling overwhelmed and uncertain. Yet, in time, I discovered a strength I never knew I had, and I've learned to treasure my loved one's memory as a source of guidance. My hope is that you, too, find ways to honor your feelings and carry your loved ones with you. Embrace the lessons, the moments of both joy and sorrow that life brings. Trust that growth often blooms from hardship. May your experience lead you to peace and understanding, just as mine has, and may you integrate your grief into the beautiful tapestry of your life.

Mom's Final Journal Entry – Saturday

(Note: The time frame was removed so you don't compare your own process to hers; as we all heal differently.)

> *"Saturday ~ It has now been XXX time that my love has been gone. It seems much longer. I'm getting further with the therapist. Met Tammy and her husband last weekend in Scottsdale. You can only imagine how nice it was. I gather great strength from them. They always make me feel so included!*
>
> *That means so much!*

I think it's time for me to move on ... I need to go out and find me after all these years."

Mom pulled another KindNotes that said: "**No matter how you feel, get up, dress up, show up, and never give up**."

Discover the path that only you can walk and embrace your grief along the way. May this journal remain a steadfast companion long after you've closed this book.

CHAPTER ELEVEN

CONCLUSION

MY LETTER TO MY DAD

To my dad,

Your unwavering strength and willingness to teach me, whether it was oil changes, fixing tires, or even mending Barbie dolls, have been the foundation of my life. You've always been my guiding light, showing me that I was capable of more than I ever imagined. Though you may not be here to read this, I want to honor the lasting influence you've had on my journey.

Thank you for always being there for us in our times of need. Your love and support have never gone unnoticed. This book reflects the invaluable lessons I've learned and continue to learn, since your passing: lessons of resilience, hope, and the courage to embrace life's changes.

Thank you for believing in me, for every piece of advice, and for being a constant presence in my life. Words can never fully capture what you mean to me. Your love and guidance have shaped who I am, and I'll forever be grateful for that. The strength and love you gave to Mom continue to hold us all together. We love you more than words can ever convey, and your impact will stay with us always.

Dad, your legacy inspired me to share these stories and lessons. And through this work, I strive to honor the love and light you brought into our lives. Thank you.

With all my love,

Your daughter

John & Tammy

CHAPTER TWELVE

ACKNOWLEDGMENT

Writing this book has been an intensely personal and transformative journey—one that would not have been possible without the love, guidance, and support of so many incredible individuals. I am deeply grateful to the grief counselors, writers, and thought leaders whose wisdom has illuminated the path of loss, healing, and memory. While this book is born from my personal experiences, it has been shaped by the insights of those who have walked this journey before me.

A heartfelt thank you to my editorial team and everyone who reviewed this manuscript. Your thoughtful feedback and encouragement helped shape these pages in ways I couldn't have done alone.

To my writing coach, **Michael Jaymes**—thank you for your steady guidance and belief in my story. Your encouragement helped give voice to emotions I didn't always know how to put into words. But you've been so much more than a writing coach. You've shared your knowledge generously, offered your connections without hesitation, and reminded me that this story was worth telling. Your impact has shaped both this book and the writer I've become—and for that, I'll always be thankful.

To those who have shared their grief experiences with me: You've shown me the power of connection and the incredible resilience we all possess. Thank you for trusting me with your most personal and meaningful moments.

SPECIAL SUPPORTERS

Your generosity helped make this project possible. I am especially grateful to the following individuals for their support and belief in this book's mission:

- Laura Sustrik
- Bob Miller
- Frank Cortez
- Laura Maynes Cortez

Gratefully acknowledging the incredible support of:

- **Stephany Arruda**, your encouragement and support were a bright light throughout this process. Thank you for believing in me and the message behind these pages.
- **Vanessa Geller**, thank you for listening to me in my tough times, for the tears, and the "let's get lunch" invites which allowed me to get out of the house and remember life. I am so grateful to have you in my life.

EXECUTIVE CONTRIBUTOR

- **Anthony Cortez**, thank you for the incredible role you played in bringing this dream to life. I'll never forget the moment I said, "I think I'm going to write a book," and without hesitation, you smiled and said, "That's going to be great for you." You believed in me from the very beginning, without question. Your strength, encouragement, and steady presence gave me the confidence to keep going—especially on the days when I wasn't sure I could. Having you by my side has meant more than words can express. I truly couldn't have done this without you. Thank you so much, I love you! xxooxx – me

Finally, I extend my deepest gratitude to the readers of this book. By sharing my journey, I hope to offer you companionship and hope as you navigate your own experience of loss.

REFLECTIONS THROUGH WRITING A GUIDE TO YOUR JOURNALING MEMORIES

Journaling can be one of the most powerful tools for navigating grief and life transitions. In the pages that follow, you will find ample space to write freely. There is no right or wrong way to journal; the most important step is simply beginning. Allow these blank pages to become a mirror for your inner world, a safe place where you can be honest, vulnerable, and unafraid to rewrite your own narrative of loss and renewal.

Take your time. Whether you write daily, weekly, or only when the need arises, each entry is a meaningful step toward understanding, acceptance, and growth. May this journaling section serve as a personal refuge for self-discovery and as a testament to the enduring love that continues to guide you forward.

Now that we've explored the lessons in these pages, it's time to put pen to paper and uncover your own reflections. May each entry you write soothe your sorrow and spark new understanding. And if you find yourself needing more guidance, I invite you to follow me beyond this book.

Together, we can continue sharing hope and healing one step at a time.

WHAT COMES AFTER THE JOURNAL

After completing the journal section, be sure to explore the additional resources that follow. You'll find:

- Helpful References
- Research & Educational Sources
- Grief and Online Communities
- Therapy & Immediate Support Options
- Tools and Healing Resources
- Professional Contributions
- About the Author

These sections are here to support your continued reflection, provide expert insight, and connect you to compassionate communities and helpful tools.

YOUR JOURNAL

"Your Thoughts,

Your Way.

Write Freely, Without Judgment."

Date

Journal Notes – Use this space to expand your personal reflections

Date

Date

Journal Notes – Use this space to expand your personal reflections

Date

Journal Notes – Use this space to expand your personal reflections

Date

Date

Journal Notes – Use this space to expand your personal reflections

Date

Journal Notes – Use this space to expand your personal reflections

Date

Journal Notes – Use this space to expand your personal reflections

Date

Journal Notes – Use this space to expand your personal reflections

Date

Journal Notes – Use this space to expand your personal reflections

Date

Date

Journal Notes – Use this space to expand your personal reflections

Date

Date

Journal Notes – Use this space to expand your personal reflections

Date

Date

Journal Notes – Use this space to expand your personal reflections

Date

Journal Notes – Use this space to expand your personal reflections

Date

Journal Notes – Use this space to expand your personal reflections

Date

Date

Journal Notes – Use this space to expand your personal reflections

Date

Journal Notes – Use this space to expand your personal reflections

Date

Journal Notes – Use this space to expand your personal reflections

Date

Journal Notes – Use this space to expand your personal reflections

Date

Journal Notes – Use this space to expand your personal reflections

Date

Date

Date

Journal Notes – Use this space to expand your personal reflections

Date

Journal Notes – Use this space to expand your personal reflections

Date

Journal Notes – Use this space to expand your personal reflections

Date

Journal Notes – Use this space to expand your personal reflections

Date

Date

Journal Notes – Use this space to expand your personal reflections

Date

Date

Journal Notes – Use this space to expand your personal reflections

Date

Journal Notes – Use this space to expand your personal reflections

Date

Journal Notes – Use this space to expand your personal reflections

Date

Date

Journal Notes – Use this space to expand your personal reflections

Date

Date

Journal Notes – Use this space to expand your personal reflections

Date

Journal Notes – Use this space to expand your personal reflections

Date

Journal Notes – Use this space to expand your personal reflections

Date

Journal Notes – Use this space to expand your personal reflections

Date

Journal Notes – Use this space to expand your personal reflections

Date

Journal Notes – Use this space to expand your personal reflections

Date

Journal Notes – Use this space to expand your personal reflections

Date

Date

Journal Notes – Use this space to expand your personal reflections

Date

Journal Notes – Use this space to expand your personal reflections

Date

Journal Notes – Use this space to expand your personal reflections

Date

Date

Date

Journal Notes – Use this space to expand your personal reflections

Date

Journal Notes – Use this space to expand your personal reflections

Date

Journal Notes – Use this space to expand your personal reflections

Date

Journal Notes – Use this space to expand your personal reflections

Date

Journal Notes – Use this space to expand your personal reflections

Date

Journal Notes – Use this space to expand your personal reflections

Date

Date

Journal Notes – Use this space to expand your personal reflections

REFLECTION THROUGH WRITING | 193

Date

Journal Notes – Use this space to expand your personal reflections

Date

Journal Notes – Use this space to expand your personal reflections

Date

Journal Notes – Use this space to expand your personal reflections

Date

Journal Notes – Use this space to expand your personal reflections

REFLECTION THROUGH WRITING

Date

Journal Notes – Use this space to expand your personal reflections

Date

Journal Notes – Use this space to expand your personal reflections

Date

Journal Notes – Use this space to expand your personal reflections

Date

Journal Notes – Use this space to expand your personal reflections

Date

Date

Journal Notes – Use this space to expand your personal reflections

Date

Journal Notes – Use this space to expand your personal reflections

Date

Date

Journal Notes – Use this space to expand your personal reflections

Date

Journal Notes – Use this space to expand your personal reflections

Date

Date

Journal Notes – Use this space to expand your personal reflections

Date

Journal Notes – Use this space to expand your personal reflections

Date

Journal Notes – Use this space to expand your personal reflections

Date

Journal Notes – Use this space to expand your personal reflections

Date

Journal Notes – Use this space to expand your personal reflections

Date

Journal Notes – Use this space to expand your personal reflections

Date

Journal Notes – Use this space to expand your personal reflections

Date

Journal Notes – Use this space to expand your personal reflections

Date

Date

Journal Notes – Use this space to expand your personal reflections

Date

Journal Notes – Use this space to expand your personal reflections

Date

Journal Notes – Use this space to expand your personal reflections

Date

Date

Date

Date

Date

Journal Notes – Use this space to expand your personal reflections

REFLECTION THROUGH WRITING | 225

Date

Journal Notes – Use this space to expand your personal reflections

Date

Journal Notes – Use this space to expand your personal reflections

Date

Journal Notes – Use this space to expand your personal reflections

Date

Date

Date

Date

Journal Notes – Use this space to expand your personal reflections

Date

Journal Notes – Use this space to expand your personal reflections

Date

Journal Notes – Use this space to expand your personal reflections

Date

Journal Notes – Use this space to expand your personal reflections

Date

Date

Journal Notes – Use this space to expand your personal reflections

Date

Journal Notes – Use this space to expand your personal reflections

Date

Date

Journal Notes – Use this space to expand your personal reflections

Date

Journal Notes – Use this space to expand your personal reflections

Date

Date

Journal Notes – Use this space to expand your personal reflections

Date

Journal Notes – Use this space to expand your personal reflections

Date

Journal Notes – Use this space to expand your personal reflections

Date

Journal Notes – Use this space to expand your personal reflections

Date

Journal Notes – Use this space to expand your personal reflections

Date

Date

Journal Notes – Use this space to expand your personal reflections

Date

Date

Journal Notes – Use this space to expand your personal reflections

Date

Date

Journal Notes – Use this space to expand your personal reflections

Date

Date

Journal Notes – Use this space to expand your personal reflections

Date

Journal Notes – Use this space to expand your personal reflections

Date

Date

Date

Journal Notes – Use this space to expand your personal reflections

Date

Date

Journal Notes – Use this space to expand your personal reflections

Date

Journal Notes – Use this space to expand your personal reflections

Date

Journal Notes – Use this space to expand your personal reflections

REFLECTION THROUGH WRITING | 263

Date

Journal Notes – Use this space to expand your personal reflections

Date

Journal Notes – Use this space to expand your personal reflections

Date

Journal Notes – Use this space to expand your personal reflections

Date

Journal Notes – Use this space to expand your personal reflections

Date

Journal Notes – Use this space to expand your personal reflections

Date

Journal Notes – Use this space to expand your personal reflections

REFLECTION THROUGH WRITING | 269

Date

Journal Notes – Use this space to expand your personal reflections

Date

Journal Notes – Use this space to expand your personal reflections

Date

Date

Journal Notes – Use this space to expand your personal reflections

Date

Date

Date

Date

Journal Notes – Use this space to expand your personal reflections

Date

Journal Notes – Use this space to expand your personal reflections

Date

Journal Notes – Use this space to expand your personal reflections

Date

Journal Notes – Use this space to expand your personal reflections

Date

Journal Notes – Use this space to expand your personal reflections

Date

Journal Notes – Use this space to expand your personal reflections

Date

Journal Notes – Use this space to expand your personal reflections

Date

Journal Notes – Use this space to expand your personal reflections

Date

Journal Notes – Use this space to expand your personal reflections

Date

Date

Journal Notes – Use this space to expand your personal reflections

Date

Journal Notes – Use this space to expand your personal reflections

Date

Date

Journal Notes – Use this space to expand your personal reflections

Date

Date

Journal Notes – Use this space to expand your personal reflections

Date

Date

Date

Journal Notes – Use this space to expand your personal reflections

Date

Date

Date

Journal Notes – Use this space to expand your personal reflections

Date

Journal Notes – Use this space to expand your personal reflections

Date

Journal Notes – Use this space to expand your personal reflections

Date

Journal Notes – Use this space to expand your personal reflections

Date

Journal Notes – Use this space to expand your personal reflections

Date

Journal Notes – Use this space to expand your personal reflections

REFLECTION THROUGH WRITING | 303

Date

Journal Notes – Use this space to expand your personal reflections

Date

Journal Notes – Use this space to expand your personal reflections

Date

Journal Notes – Use this space to expand your personal reflections

Date

Journal Notes – Use this space to expand your personal reflections

Date

Journal Notes – Use this space to expand your personal reflections

Date

Journal Notes – Use this space to expand your personal reflections

Date

Journal Notes – Use this space to expand your personal reflections

Date

Journal Notes – Use this space to expand your personal reflections

Date

Date

Date

Journal Notes – Use this space to expand your personal reflections

Date

Journal Notes – Use this space to expand your personal reflections

Date

Journal Notes – Use this space to expand your personal reflections

Date

Date

Date

Journal Notes — Use this space to expand your personal reflections

Date

Journal Notes – Use this space to expand your personal reflections

Date

Date

Journal Notes – Use this space to expand your personal reflections

Date

Date

Journal Notes – Use this space to expand your personal reflections

Date

Date

Journal Notes – Use this space to expand your personal reflections

Date

Date

Date

Journal Notes – Use this space to expand your personal reflections

Date

Date

Journal Notes – Use this space to expand your personal reflections

Date

Date

Journal Notes – Use this space to expand your personal reflections

Date

Date

Journal Notes – Use this space to expand your personal reflections

Date

Journal Notes – Use this space to expand your personal reflections

Date

Date

Date

Journal Notes – Use this space to expand your personal reflections

REFERENCES

This book is based on my personal experiences and insights, shaped by the love, loss, and healing I've encountered along the way. While every story shared is my own, I've also drawn from a variety of trusted resources that have helped deepen my understanding of grief.

If you're seeking additional support or want to continue exploring these topics, the following references were especially meaningful in the creation of this book—and may offer comfort, guidance, and insight as you continue your own journey:

RESEARCH AND EDUCATIONAL SOURCES

- **Medical News Today** – "Stages of Grief": This article provided foundational insights into the emotional stages of grief and how they manifest.
- **National Library of Medicine** – "Kubler-Ross Stages of Dying and Subsequent Models of Grief": This reference explored the widely recognized models of grief and their evolving interpretations.

- **Tides Program** – "What Not to Do When You're Grieving": This resource offered practical advice on navigating grief and avoiding common pitfalls.

GRIEF SUPPORT AND ONLINE COMMUNITIES

- **Grief Share** – A national network of support groups for those coping with loss. griefshare.org
- **Help Guide** – Coping with grief and loss tips and practical advice. helpguide.org
- **Modern Loss** – Online community featuring articles, personal stories, and resources. modernloss.com
- **Psychology Today** – Grief articles and support tools. psychologytoday.com
- **The Compassionate Friends** – Support for families grieving the loss of a child. compassionatefriends.org

THERAPY AND IMMEDIATE SUPPORT

- **Better Help** – Online counseling sessions with licensed therapists. betterhelp.com
- **National Suicide Prevention Lifeline** – For urgent emotional support: 1-800-273-8255 or suicidepreventionlifeline.org

TOOLS AND RESOURCES

- **KindNotes, Inc.®** – A heartfelt tool for offering emotional support through uplifting messages. KindNotes.com

- **OpenAI** – Assisted in developing clarity within the text and contributed to the cover image design.

PERSONAL CONTRIBUTIONS

- **Laura Maynes Cortez, MSW** *(Master of Science in Social Work)* – This advanced degree means she is specially trained in understanding human behavior, emotional well-being, and the challenges individuals and families face during difficult life transitions.

MSW professionals are often on the front lines of emotional support—offering guidance, advocating for vulnerable communities, and helping people heal through grief, trauma, and major life changes. Their insights draw from both research and real-world experience, making their perspective an invaluable part of this work.

I'm incredibly grateful for her thoughtful review and the heart she brought to this project.

- **Rachel Mostofizadeh** – A storyteller photographer specializing in lifestyle storytelling. She can be found on Facebook and Instagram or contacted at rachel@rachelelizphoto.com.

NOTE ON RESOURCES AND ACKNOWLEDGMENTS

The exercises and content in this book have been carefully reviewed and developed with the assistance of AI to ensure clarity and relevance. A full review has also been completed by professionals in the field. None of the resources listed have compensated me for their inclusion, and all content references remain with the original authors and owners.

Now for the legal stuff: The lawyers would want me to say this book is based on my own personal experiences, reflections, and research. I'm not a doctor, therapist, lawyer, or anyone with credentials to tell you what to do or how to feel. Only you know what's right for you. And if you're not sure, that's okay too. There's absolutely nothing wrong with reaching out to a licensed professional for support.

My hope is that something in my story speaks to you and that even just a part of this book helps you feel seen, supported, and a little less alone in your grief. If it brings you even one step closer to healing, then sharing it was more than worth it.

Thank you to those whose work has contributed to this journey of healing.

The author and publisher are not responsible for the content found on third-party websites or referenced sources. While all links, resources, and references listed in this book were current at the time of publication, the digital landscape changes rapidly. We cannot guarantee that external content will remain accurate, accessible, or unchanged. The author receives no compensation or endorsement benefit from any third-party inclusion

Again, if grief becomes overwhelming and you need immediate support, reach out for help.

National Suicide Prevention Lifeline:

1-800-273-8255

or

https://suicidepreventionlifeline.org/

ABOUT THE AUTHOR

Tammy Cortez, is a wife, mom, daughter, sister, and lifelong learner who never expected to write a book about grief. But after losing her dad, the weight of that loss pushed her into a new kind of reflection, one that brought healing through writing, storytelling, and connection.

Professionally, Tammy spent her career in Learning and Development, helping people grow, lead, and adapt through life's changes. Personally, she has always believed that love and loss are deeply intertwined, and that grief doesn't mean we're broken; it means we've loved deeply.

Generations of Grief wasn't written because Tammy had all the answers. It was written because she didn't! Tammy needed to find her way forward. Through journal entries, memories, and moments of grace, she has learned that we carry the people we've lost into every part of our future. This book is her way of honoring that truth and inviting others to do the same.

Tammy believes healing is possible, growth is ongoing, and while the journey can feel lonely at times, we are never truly alone.

ALSO AVAILABLE

Looking for a more personal touch? A signed **Keepsake Edition** of *Generations of Grief: Embracing Change Through Loss* is available—a beautifully crafted hardcover, personally signed by the author. Designed for gift-giving and deeper reflection, this special edition features an upgraded dust jacket and makes a meaningful way to honor your grief journey or share it with someone you love.

Order your signed copy at: www.tammylcortez.com

CONNECT WITH ME

Thank you for allowing *Generations of Grief: Embracing Change Through Loss* to be part of your healing. If this book brought you comfort, insight, or hope, I'd love to stay in touch.

You can find me here:
Website: www.TammyLCortez.com
LinkedIn: www.linkedin.com/in/tammylcortez

Follow Along:
Instagram: @tammylcortez
Facebook: facebook.com/TammyLCortez71

Your story continues!
Thank you for letting me be part of it.

Grief may shape us,

but it doesn't define us!

There is always hope

waiting on the other side.

This page intentionally left blank

www.ingramcontent.com/pod-product-compliance
Lightning Source LLC
Chambersburg PA
CBHW050526100526
44581CB00009B/151/J